*In loving memory of my great- grandma,
Mary Lee Stiff*

Prologue

When I'm on the field, I'm at peace with myself. It's just the ball and me, everything else becomes irrelevant. There's no pain from the outside world, no problems, no concerns, just me, I don't feel anything else. The moment I take off my cleats everything find its way back. That same aggravating weight lands right back on my shoulders, but I just deal with it. My great- grandmother once told me facing all my problems will build my character.

I always ask myself why? Why do I love this game so much? What is it about this game that I can't get enough of? What keeps me coming back over and over again once I've been hurt? My heart has all the answers and I only know one speed: full.

In life you can either live your dreams or you can live your fears and allow those fears to hold you back from becoming the person you want to be. In this jungle you get one shot and if you miss, you become prey in an open field surrounded by the hungry. The only way to get ahead of the game, and even life, is to separate yourself from every other athlete and get started with what you want to accomplish right now; tomorrow might be too late.

No matter how bad it is, no matter how bad it gets, I'm going to make it. I hate excuses, they don't exist in my world, they're just something to make you feel better. In life you will most likely become what you think about the most.

It's the feeling of the ball that I'm addicted to. Meanwhile, one –on- one coverages, one- hand grabs, screen plays, deep routes, loud yelling and everything else about football gives me butterflies.

Pregame

    I'm Rajon Rodgers, the Man, and football might be my only way out. It seems I have a natural aptitude for football. My objective is to make a living off of this sport as soon as possible. I have big dreams, I'm talking humongous! Not to mention my heart is even bigger than any dream I've ever dreamt.

    I am a slot and outside receiver at West Wood High School on the untamed south side of Chicago. Nobody's safe here in this neighborhood, not even the youth, and that's the sad part if you ask me. I'm highly respected at West Wood, and everywhere else around my city.

    Everyone calls me Clutch. It's not rocket science why they call me that, it appears from the way I play on the gridiron. I'm a six foot 170 pound beast with pure skill and ability. I've never come across a single individual that was better than I am. Superman is good, I mean he's huge, powerful, and I bet he's even quick on his feet. Batman is great, and he's my favorite superhero, but on the football field those two are useless against me. They might be fiction super heroes who can save the world, but if they're in cleats standing in front of me, I would definitely terminate them both.

    I'm quick, quicker than the blink of an eye. I'm dangerous, more dangerous than a four-year- old holding an open bottle of poison. I'm a dog, I'm *Cujo*. I'm a lion, a hungry one. I'm a beast, a greedy beast, there's no beauty in me.

My catching ability is perilous. Coaches have told me over the years that I have a great set of hands, just throw me the ball, plain and simple. When my team needs a first down I can make it, if we ever get into an arduous dogfight, I'm the one to depend on. I'm just highly competitive and poised. I wouldn't guard myself one -on -one if I were you because that's even worse than poison. If I were you, I'd make sure I even have help over the top from the free safety and when I'm hot, I suggest the corner and the safety to have help all around my area.

Don't leave me with one defender, that's risky. Double cover me, in fact, triple cover me, even defensive coaches should be cautious. I define myself as a natural born leader, play me weak and I'll beat you deep every single time. No one can stop me two plays in a row it's impossible. Guarding me and locking me down are two different situations, try guarding me before jumping to conclusions. You might knock me off my route a few times maybe, that's normal, but when I get mad, you will pay. I accept credit or debit, whichever one works best for you.

Other than this sport of football, I'm counting on my character to get far in life. Football can reveal the real you and show your true character when adversity sets in. You can learn a lot from this game; things that can set you up for the real world.

My worst enemy is fatigue. The moment the

feeling of fatigue appears, it can easily change someone performance within a split second. Being mentally strong is the best cure ever. I have an uncontrolled hunger for success and the mindset of a winner. I will never settle or accept anything less I worked hard for, that's just who I am.

I'm not a fan of sleeping in, especially in the summer time. Sleep is for those who don't have an urge to be successful in life, if really all you do is sleep through the day. There are so many different opportunities in life to grab, with sleep I'm pretty sure you will miss out on a lot. I just rest from time to time when I feel the need to.

Rise and grind is my motto. My summer is strictly about football, I don't waste my time hanging in the streets waiting to get myself killed. I wake up, blow a kiss to God and my grandmother, wash my face, and fix a small breakfast. Today it contains two pieces of toast, with a few scrapes of butter, using the last we have. I choose to always eat light so I don't eat too much before practicing. I drink a glass of orange juice, too because I hear it's good for you.

I eat while watching *Sports Center,* if my TV decides to act right. When I make it to the pros, a TV might be the first thing I buy for my mother. I brush my teeth right before I leave and head to practice.

My workouts are stressful, but I know they are improving my game. I call anyone who has a nice arm to throw me the ball and that's usually my guy Tank from down the street. He has a gun for an arm and he doesn't even play quarterback. Who knows where his strong arm comes from? I have one guess, but I would rather keep it to myself so I don't embarrass him. Tank used to play quarterback for a school called Cordale High but he punched some kid and got kicked out so there goes his one- way ticket out of this neighborhood. Either way, when I make it I'll pay him to throw me passes during my off season. I usually meet him on his corner or once in a while we just meet on the field.

    I like to lace up my cleats while listening to my music, I prefer something to get me hyped, like rap. It helps me focus as I walk onto the field with an intensive look on my face. Usually he shows up while I'm still putting my cleats on, but by the time Tank arrives today, I'm in the middle of the field stretching.

    Today he's a little late for some reason, probably getting that arm strong I bet. By the time he finally comes onto the field I'm doing cone drills, still listening to music. We don't really talk much before we practice, we just get ready to put some good work in. We start off by him warming up his shoulder and I warm up my hands by catching without gloves. Gloves are just for fashion on the field, I usually use gloves to give my sweaty hands a little support with a little better grip. Either way it goes, I still have the best hands around.

    I thought I was Mr. Cool Guy last year when I played in the game without gloves and my finger got jammed real bad; I learned my lesson then. After warm ups we get right into my routes. My favorite routes are fades, posts, and screen passes.

It really doesn't matter how you throw the ball when I'm training, just throw it and I'll go get it. I try to train myself to be a humble, triple threat receiver. I'll beat you deep, short, mid-field, or wherever the ball is thrown, no matter what, I'm going up for it.

In Chicago it's never quiet outside, I mean never, even when it's raining outside. There are always a few drunks, low lives, or drug dealers stopping by the field that I train on, they really just watch and say stuff like, "Keep working 'Lil homie," or "Your hard work is gonna pay off shorty," "Make sure you don't forget where you came from once you blow up."

In my eyes it's all just motivation. It makes me want to run my routes harder and catch the ball more aggressively, even catch the most difficult passes that people might think I'm not able to grab. I love when someone claps, if I know who it's coming from, I might point to that person or give them a fist pump for a sign of gratitude. I'm a show off.

After a while I see more people stand around to watch, so now it's time for me to put on an even better show. After some light route running, I gave Tank a nod to let him know it's clutch time. He smirked and caught the ball when I tossed it back to him. Jogging back to the line I see more people come to watch; this is getting good. Blood rushing through my veins, I want to do something spectacular. I got into my receiver stance and looked over at Tank breathing with composure.

Tank shouted, "Ready!" He yelled it out loud enough for the whole park to hear, "Set go!"

I took off immediately once I heard, "set."

Full speed, I fake with a jab step like I was running a quick slant and I went on a fade route. Tank released the ball after three seconds, the ball rides through the air looking like it's about six yards ahead of me. I hit a second gear of speed and looked over my shoulder cautiously for the ball. I took a four- yard leap and smack! The ball lands between the Nike symbols on my gloves as my body hits the warm, thick grass. I caught the ball with every inch of my fingertips and I made sure I hugged it while going down, a natural feeling. I hear clapping all around me.

"That young boy is good!" Someone in the crowd shouted.

As always, I gave the crowd my famous fist pump. Tank was geeked about my catch. I raced back and we met up in the air for a manly body bump.

For about forty five more minutes of running routes and catching passes, I was ready for a shower, something to eat and drink, and a short nap to refresh my body. Tank and I walked down Loomis Boulevard, which is the long way home. That's when we usually talk since it's all about business when we first meet up.

"What you on for the rest of the day Bro?" He asked.

"Nothing man, I got practice at 3:00 at the school," I replied.

"Aw yeah, I forgot about that," he said. "So are you ready for the season or what?"

I don't even know why he would even ask me some bull shit like that.

"Is a new born fish ready for water or what?" I asked. "Hell yeah I'm ready to ball!" As I beat my chest with my fists. "I'm not the one you should be asking that to. Any corner who has to sit in front of me this season is gonna be disappointed, just wait on it!"

"I hear you bruh, I hear you," Tank agreed

"Alright Bro just hit me up when you trying to get some more work in," I said.

"You bet!" Tank claimed.

After separating, I put my head phones back on and made my way home. It's actually kind of dangerous doing that in a neighborhood like mine, but everyone knows who Clutch is so if a fool tries to rob me, he better live on the other side of town or somewhere far away, but good luck, because I don't fold easy. You might just have to kill me. I turned my music down as I got close to the crib and heard people calling out to me:

"Yooo Clutch!"

"My main man Clutch!"

"Clutch!"

"Touch down Clutch!"

"First round pick"

"Clutch Rodgers!"

    I enjoy all the hype, it makes me laugh. I just give them dap and keep going. I live in an ancient tall, brown wooden building right next to a barber shop that has been there for over 60 years. It's been there for so long that I bet Martin Luther King stopped by for a haircut during the Civil Rights era.

    When I got upstairs, Dee Dee was watching her favorite television show. She's my six- year-old sister that I love to death and would take a bullet for any given day. I'm going have a lot of trouble with these little punk boys around here when she gets older. She has a smooth, caramel complexion, curly brown hair, chocolate chip cookie brown eyes, and the most stunning smile with dimples, and she's a little hoop star. She knows I will always be there for her no matter what.

    All Mom does is work, it seems like she wakes up and goes to work, comes home from work, sleeps a little then wakes back up and does it all over again. She's a working machine. I thank God for giving me such a special, unique woman. My mother has been there for me since birth. I remember the day I had surgery on my middle finger, she sat there through the whole operation from the time it started until it was finished. There was also another time I had surgery on my toe and when I woke up she was the first person my eyes were attached to.

My mother kept me lifted my whole entire life, drying tears from my face and making me feel how a mother should make her child feel. She's my motivation and one of the reasons why I grind the way I do. My job is to get my mother and little sister away from this environment the first opportunity I get. I want to close my eyes and turn my back without worrying about them. It's dangerous out here, it's a war. Every ball I catch is for them, not forgetting my great- grandma.

I lost my great- grandma when I was in the fifth grade. She was one of my biggest motivations and still is. She departed from this earth but will always and forever live in my heart. I cherish her spirit daily and use the memory of her to influence my game on the field, she's another reason why I breathe. I used to live with her when I was little before Dee Dee was born. It's safe to say I was spoiled, I got almost everything I ever wanted as a kid. She wasn't just any ordinary great-grandma, she was my teacher of compassion, of love and fearlessness. She was more than my best friend, better than my coach, more like my provider, my heart beat, she was my everything.

The day she died I felt like I was wiped out. I didn't know my purpose for living anymore. I remember the day of her funeral like it was yesterday. I sat there in the front row in complete shock. She kept me balanced throughout my whole childhood. The things I'm able to do are because of her like cooking, cleaning, reading, writing, and just being a strong, young man.

One summer evening, I ran into the house crying because someone hit me with a stick. My grandma sent me back outside and made me stand up for myself. I knocked the boy off his bike and broke his stick into pieces. My grandma taught me how to be tough, she taught me that life is always going to hit hard and after falling, you have to get up and hit back even harder with more force than you were hit with. I know she's looking down from heaven and smiling every time I make a touchdown.

All touchdowns are dedicated to her, Mom and Dee Dee. Family is everything to me. My father is not a part of my life anymore, I deem him worthless. In fact, I really don't know what he's worth since he's not in my life. When I was around the age of five years old he took me shopping at Wal-Mart just a few days after my birthday had passed. He let me pick out all these different toys, telling me that I can have anything I wanted. There was a bench in the store I'll never forget. He took a small piece of paper and put it in my left hand telling me to keep a tight grip on it until he gets back while he went to pick out the biggest toy ever. He told me not to move. I felt like the luckiest kid in the world while I sat there waiting on him for hours with a smile on my face.

I was asked by store managers over and over again, "Where are your parents?"

All I could tell them is what he had me thinking the whole entire time.

I told them, "My dad is picking me out a toy."

Even after the store closed I just knew my father was somewhere lost in the store trying to carry my toy to where he left me.

The police took me in and questioned me for at least two whole hours. I was waiting on my dad to come rescue me with my toy. A police officer opened my hand and took the piece of paper away from me, it had my mother's phone number on it. I haven't seen my father since. I don't think I can ever forgive him, I still think about him daily, though.

There are only a few things I remember about him, other than the fact that he left a major hole in my heart; I don't have a clue how he could ever make up for his poor actions. Words and money can't fix the damage he has done by not being there as I grew up. It's the fact that the years he missed in my life when I needed him there the most. I feel like every kid needs their father in their life. A father is everything to a kid. I wish he knew how good I was, I wish he came to my games and watched me from the bleachers.

Every time I hear a man's voice coming from the crowd, I hope it's him with that toy he promised. I hope it's my father looking right at me with a huge smile on his face. A dream I have that will never come true is my dad training me. I wish he woke me up in the mornings and made me work my butt off, I want to be pushed by my dad, I want him to yell at me when I drop the ball or run the wrong route. I want him to help me stay away from distractions and make me remain focused, instead he's somewhere else living his own life. He might even be in jail. I doubt that my pops knows anything about football. Even if he doesn't like sports, the least he could do is grab me and hold me tight in his arms letting me know he has my back.

Meanwhile, Dee Dee's dad is pretty cool. He comes around twice every other week to either drop off money or food. He's a big time drug dealer so he's not allowed in our apartment building. My mother doesn't even want him to pass the downstairs door bell, she thinks there are a lot of people after him, which I think she might be right about that. He always tells me to look after my little sister, which I always do, so him telling me that is very irrelevant to my ears. Dee Dee is smart enough to sit in the house without burning it down when Mom and I are away for a few hours.

Our hot water wasn't on so after taking a cold shower, I searched everywhere for food in the kitchen. I ran through the cabinets like I haven't eaten in years, I need food in my stomach.

"Mom left money on the counter for food," Dee Dee said.

"Perfect, I'll bring home dinner after practice then," I told her. "Will you be good until then?"

"Yeah I'll be fine," she replied.

We ate some stale noodles and took a nap together. After a few hours went by, it was getting close to practice, the moment I've been waiting for. Mark called me as soon as I woke up to see what time I was leaving out.

Mark is like another brother to me. He's always been someone I could depend on. We've always had each other's back no matter what. He plays receiver also. We became good friends in the seventh grade and have been tight since then. His problems become my problems without a doubt. After getting dressed, I grabbed my black duffel bag, kissed Dee Dee on the forehead, and walked out the door. The weather is pretty nice today, nice enough to push myself to be great. I pray to God daily that we don't get rain. I decided to stop by the corner store to get a cold Gatorade before meeting Mark. He was waiting for me three blocks down towards the school.

"Man it's hotter than a fat girl's bellybutton!" he said.

I started laughing because of the facial expression he made. This is one funny guy.

"Man let's go before we're late," I said.

We made predictions about how practice was going to turn out.

As we got closer to the school, we saw Jerry and his dirty gang. If you're going to talk about bums, Jerry and his gang are some of the biggest ones. I don't trust any of them, in fact, I wouldn't even ask them for directions. Those guys are major thieves. They will steal anything they can get their hands on: iPhones, money, clothes, doorbells, car rims, and anything else that's valuable to them. They even break into houses, cars, garages, and anything else with a door. I'm pretty sure they would steal grass out of someone's backyard if it looked different from everyone else's.

They also start fights and like to jump people. When they saw us we shook their hands and kept walking. Jerry has never given me trouble out of all the years I've known him, it's like he has some type of respect for me. I mean, if he ever took it there with me then I wouldn't have a problem finishing the situation. I'm pretty sure Jerry wouldn't even be able to handle a guy like me, these hands move too quick for him.

"Yo Mark check it out real quick Bro!" Jerry yelled.

I stopped to wait on him. They talked for one whole minute then Mark walked away.

"What did he want Mark?" I asked him.

 "Oh nothing really," he said.

"Yeah ok, don't get yourself in any mess boy!" I warned him.

"I'm not," he replied.

When we arrived at the school our teammates

were all walking in together. All of them were wearing our team shirts and shorts, wearing book bags. Our colors are smoke grey, black, and gold. West Wood High is known for good athletes and the best uniforms. We have black speed revolution helmets, with smoke grey face masks with our numbers printed gold on the back. My number is one.

Daniel, PJ, Chris and Bertron saw us the moment we arrived on school grounds. Betron is my quarterback, he's just good, point-blank period. We all start on offense, Bertron is the quarterback. I'm at receiver, along with PJ, Chris, and Mark. Daniel plays running back, he's about 5'7" and stocky. That man has pure speed, in the open field, you will not be even close to catching him, even if you're good. I wish you the best of luck because he's very explosive and will run over anything in his way.

It's safe to say I'm Bertron's number one target, he said it himself one day at practice. When he's in danger I come back to the ball for a decent catch and turn it into big yards or six points. PJ is really good too if, you are one- on- one with him he will make your knees touch the ground along with your elbow and hands, meaning he's a great athlete. Chris is about 6'3" 189 pounds, if you throw the ball up, he will come down with it. These guys are like my brothers. I trust them, I love them, and I just enjoy competing with these knuckle heads on Friday nights.

We all went into the school locker room to get dressed for practice. The smell of our huge locker room gives me chills.

Coach White came downstairs beating on the lockers yelling, "Let's go-o-o-o, you got 10 minutes to get out there on the field ready and dressed to go."

    Coach White is the defensive coach; he even looks like a defensive coach. He's about six feet tall, brown skin, a bald head, and he always wears tight shirts to show off his muscles. He knows everything there is to know about football. If you are someone who likes to go around and hit, then you and Coach White will become best friends. The easiest way to get on his good side is to send someone off the field in a stretcher, which means you can't be scared to lay your pads down. He makes very good predictions about a play the team is about to run before they even attempt it. I put on my headphones and turned it up all the way to the max. After my cleats are on, I put on my shoulder pads followed by the rest of my uniform. I like my back plate to hang out of my practice jersey, style is everything on the field. I separate myself on the field with style and skill. After getting dressed, I grabbed my helmet, closed my locker, and then walked out to the practice field.

    The sun is still out and shining, birds are chirping, and I'm ready to practice. After we stretched as a team, we broke off into groups and warmed up. The receivers run routes, catch passes, and practice running goal line fades toward the end zone. The running backs run through cones and speed ladders, they also practice on handoffs. Our linemen push big heavy bags and focus on blocking. For me to do my job well, I start with them too. In order for my quarterback to deliver me the rock, the big uglies, I have to keep him protected. Our defense is on the other practice field focusing on what they do best.

Coach Louie blew the whistle three times after 35 minutes. That meant it was time for offense versus defense. Everyone clapped and got pumped up. It's time for somebody to either lose their starting spot or be exposed.

"First offense, first defense get out there and compete! Let's have a day guys! Compete today! Be great. Who's gonna step up today? Game day is right around the corner and I don't think South Wood is gonna lay down for you chumps!" Coach Louie yelled.

Coach Louie is my head coach and he's the only coach I ever met with a nice hairline. He's about 6'1," 230 pounds, with brown skin, low fade, trimmed beard, and the best decision maker in the world as a football coach. I honestly think he should coach in the NFL. It's like he has the power to make each and every last one of us believe in ourselves. His style of dressing is pretty cool also, he's well known for matching tennis shoes and jogging suits.

His style of coaching inspires me to want to be a great coach like him some day. He's been like a personal mentor to me since I was a freshman. His first year coaching at West Wood was actually my freshman year of high school. He always makes sure I'm focused and out of trouble, he's like a father figure to me.

Our first play was a pass play.

"Strong right, fake 17 post fade double smack glow!" Coach screamed

"On one, on one," Bertron said.

"Ready hit!" We all replied as one.

As I jogged over to the line, the defense was goofing around, I guess they think I'm a joke or something. I wanted to make a smart comment but remained quiet and got set. Bertron gave me the nod I was looking for, that means he's throwing it to me.

"Ready, set-go!" Bertron announced.

I took off full speed down field for a fade route. My corner, which was this guy named Allen, played seven yards off because he knew I liked to be jammed at the line. Bertron released the ball. Although Allen was holding onto my jersey before I even caught the ball, I still managed to grab hold of it.

"Good catch Clutch!" Coach Louie yelled.

My pet peeve is when a cornerback holds a receiver. I absolutely can't stand that weak shit. I understand if you can't guard me, that's your problem, just don't make yourself look even weaker than what you already are by holding me. Play me fair and square and I promise to make a man out of you.

We ran more plays and I caught more passes. The momentum of practice makes me more anxious for game day. Every ball that is thrown my way is my opportunity to push myself to a whole new level and look completely different from everyone else on the performance side. I feel as if the other receivers on my team look up to me, mainly the juniors and underclassmen.

    During our one- on- one drills I notice the way they watch me run my routes so they can add my moves to their game. I like that, learn from the best. With that being said it's truly my job to never lack because someone is leaning on me. Whenever I see a young receiver do something wrong, I pull him to the side and show him the right way of doing something. It's safe to call me an unofficial coach. Mickey, who is our running back, trucked one of our outside linebackers for a score that turned the intensity up in practice. All the receivers like to compete in practice to see who drops the most balls. It's usually either Chris or Mark but it's never PJ or me, we're the main two leading receivers on the team.

    During practice, a new guy walked onto our practice field with his dad, I'm guessing. He was about my height and size, but with dreads. Coach Louie went over to greet him and his dad. The boy with dreads was wearing a book bag with bright green shoes, I guess he was ready to practice seeing that he had a bag with him. That's perfect. I hope I get to make him look bad on his first day.

    Conditioning is the last part of practice, after we do that we have to take a knee and listen to what the coaches have to say about the way we practiced and any other motivational speech they might have in mind.

"Good practice today gentlemen," Coach Louie shouted, as we all clapped together. "Much improvement! Be here tomorrow ready to go we have a scrimmage versus Brook Dale in two weeks so we must prepare for a victory. Their defense is very good."

"So is our offense!" I blurted out.

"Also, we have a new member to our family," Louie said. "Introduce yourself Son."

The boy with dreads stepped up.

"Yo yo I'm Travis, I'm from Harlem and I play cornerback. I moved down here to Chicago with my pops to finish high school and play some ball. I like hitting and I look forward to playing with you guys and competing to chase state."

The dread head boy's dad stepped up, "Put him against your best receiver."

My heart started beating fast. I just knew Coach was going to let me at him. I'll give his ass a warm welcome.

Louie looked over at me, "I'll let you rest for this one," he whispered. "Go give him some work PJ!"

My heart slowed down. That was a good feeling knowing that Coach knows I'm the best receiver on this team. Travis put on his cleats and tied them up tight

23

along with his black and green shorts. He looked like he meant business, I like that. Bertron lined up and PJ lined up along with him. We all stood around watching Travis put on some green gloves and while spit on them. He lined up right in front of PJ, rubbing his gloves together to get a sticky grip. We all knew he was going for the jam.

"Ready, set-go!" Bertron shouted.

Travis' hands burst into PJ's chest with speed and power, making it difficult for PJ to get off the line.

I can't believe my eyes as he tried running on the outside of Travis. Travis kept his hand on PJ's hip so he could feel where he was as he searched for the ball in the air. My mouth dropped! I still can't believe my eyes, I expected way more out of PJ, the ball was even thrown perfectly. Travis grabbed the ball out the air and came down with it.

"Nice!" Coach Louie yelled.

Travis' dad pointed at him, I like their father and son connection. They both jogged back and Louie looked over at me with a smirk.

"Fun's over, go break his ass down," he whispered to me.

My teammates applauded as I got up. Everyone already knew what time it was except Travis and his father, I guess I'll reset their watch. Since Travis is new I will do the honor to introduce my game to him. I sat my helmet to the side, put on my gloves, and lined up in front of this clueless dread head.

"You gon' get this work!" I whispered to his face.

"You not catching nothing on me," he replied.

I gave Bertron a wink.

"Ready!" "Set, Go!" Bertron said, starting the play.

    I got off the line before he could even put his hands up. I faked like I was going out, then I burst to his inside smacking both of his hands the opposite direction I was going as I took off up the field. He was three yards behind me. I slanted the field for five yards, went up field two yards, then I tried to break him off hard by running a crisp out route. The dread head was out of position to even try to defend the pass. He's clueless, his feet are confused. Bertron threw the ball exactly where I wanted it. I snagged it then jogged back and tossed it to his dad.

"Clutch!" Coach Louie said.

The dread head boy came over to me. "Good route Bro," he complimented.

"Good defense," I replied to him.

    I gained a little respect for the kid at that very moment. He walked off towards his dad. I can tell from his dad's face that he was going to hear it the moment they left. I smacked hands with Coach Louie and went to the locker room. PJ had to stay and do 50 pushups for making Coach look bad. After I got dressed I talked and laughed around with my teammates for a little while.

"Ok guys let me get home to my little sister," I explained.

When I walked out, Coach Louie, the dread head, and his dad were coming into the school.

"See you tomorrow Clutch," Coach said.

"Iight Coach."

As I was walking away, I overheard Coach say to the boy's dad, "That kid is gonna take us far in the playoffs."

I kept walking, minding my business until Mark caught up with me.

"Yooo, Bro, good work today beast," he said.

"Always, you too man," I replied.

"What are you about to get into?" He asked me.

"N'un, just rest my body and ice up a little," I said.

Mark and I walked all the way home cracking jokes. We broke apart when I decided to stop by KFC and grab dinner for Dee Dee and myself, I'm starving. I walked home as fast as I could, attempting to run a little bit faster to get to this food. When I got upstairs and walked through the door, Dee Dee was asleep. She woke up once I got in the shower, but maybe she smelled the food sitting on the table. After I got out and got dressed I went into the kitchen with my towel around my neck.

"Put a shirt on monkey man," Dee Dee said.

"Did Mom call yet?" I asked.

"Yes, she called about five times since you've been gone," Dee Dee said. "She just wanted to make sure her baby is being looked after."

After eating I lied down looking at all my accomplishment awards I had hanging on my side of the wall, Dee Dee and I have to share a room. Twelve MVP awards, nine Offensive Players of the Year awards, Most Dedicated awards, Best Catch awards, Best Hands awards and a lot more that's covering the white spaces on my wall. It feels good looking at everything I did so far and knowing I have more to come yet, my goal is to win a Heisman Award.

The main thing I thought about is how many catches and touchdowns I was going to make this season. Then I thought about: How will even get a new pair of cleats and gloves for this season? Coach Louie has always been the one to get me what I needed since the first day I stepped foot in West Wood. Louie gave me the gloves and back plate that I'm using now, and a dark Nike visor.

I don't really ask Mom for too much because she's too busy paying bills and worrying about more important things, she's never home anyway. She tries her best to keep food in the house, even if she has to gather up pennies. Mom will keep food on the kitchen table no matter what.

I'll never forget the time when she paid this lady three two-liter pops to get her hair done, just because she spent her hair money on things for our apartment. Mom knows how to make it happen, to keep us happy. I just can't wait until the day I'm the reason why Mom stops working. I will not quit until my mother is able to rest, it will be a day when she will never have to pay another bill ever again and that's a promise. Until then, show me my competition, that's if I have any.

First Quarter

    A few days went by and I feel like I'm really improving myself so that I'll be a huge factor to my team this season. I still start out my mornings with a nice, long workout. Summer camp practices have been competitive but amusing at the same time. It contains the same thing every day: deep passes, hard hitting, loud yelling, lots of running, one- hand catches, cold Gatorade, green grass, blazing sun, and so much more that involves football and having the drive to be number one in the nation at my position.

    The new kid Travis has been trying to get at me for embarrassing him in front of his father last week. There would be times when after I catch the ball, he knocks it out of my hands even if the play is over. I don't look at it as being personal at all, though. I would try to get back at myself if I were him too for embarrassing me in front of my dad. At least his father supports him, I wish I had that. I would give up anything to have my dad at my practices and games.

    We have Brook Dale in a scrimmage in less than three days and they are pretty good. Their corners are not good enough to guard me, of course, so it is my honor to make their defense look awful. I enjoy playing against teams we never played before, this is our first time ever playing these guys. New competition is a beautiful thing, I try my best to be great in every aspect

I can.

I like to study my opponents, I watch film on different DBs in the NFL and college teams to see all the moves they like to make. You can always beat your opponent by out-thinking him and knowing what he's about to do before he does it, that's when you get into his head and throw him off his game. I like stuff like that, that's where mental toughness comes in. Football is way more mental than physical, this game is wonderful.

Before I knew it, it was time for the preseason scrimmage versus Brook Dale. We started on our practice field stretching, but I'm always ready to play. Suddenly three long buses pulled up and Brook Dale's team got off one by one, not even knowing what we had coming for them. I don't like to focus on the opposite team, when teams get off the bus I try not to show any interest. I'm game ready even when it's just a scrimmage, my mindset is aggressive and in a football helmet, I define myself as bloodthirsty. There has never been a day when I strapped up my helmet to lose. After we stretched, we went over plays against our own defense. Brook Dale started their stretches on the field down from us. How I know? Because they were loud enough for the whole neighborhood to hear them. That didn't scare me one bit. The bite of a dog is way louder than the bark.

Coach Louie walked down to their field and gossiped with their head coach. Brook Dale lined up and started walking towards our field with their starting

QB in the front. I have heard about him, he has a nice arm and he's very quick on his feet. That's what our defense like.

"Offense huddled up!" Coach Louie said.

That means we go out first. He must want us to really punish them bad because we almost never get in a huddle. We run a fast paced offense.

"Let's put their defense to work guys. Here we go, blue 12 X quick screen shield," Coach Louie said determinedly.

"On ready, on ready!" Bertron said.

"Hit!" We all said as one.

    I anxiously jogged to the line knowing I was getting the ball on a quick screen. I was thinking to myself, *how do I want to catch the ball? Do I want to just snag it and go, or do I want to actually focus on letting the ball sit perfectly in my hands?* We were lined up in trips, I'm in the middle, PJ on the outside, and Chris on the inside. They ran a four-three defense. Brook Dale corners lined up in front of us.

"Y'all bet not throw nothing my way!" Brook Dale corner yelled. "Don't you hear me talking punk?"

    My corner played about five yards off. He had so much mouth but I knew what to do to shut him up quickly, let's just say I hope he's wearing ankle braces. I want to see if I can bag up all of the smack he's talking.

31

Their linebackers bumped over to our trip's side. I felt like their whole defense knew I was getting the ball just from their concentration to my area. The free safety came over the top for anything deep.

"Down!" Bertron screeched. "Ready!"

The ball was snapped. I ran two yards up, two yards back and looked for the ball. Smack! It was a bullet pass, it felt like Bertron threw it at 200 miles per hour. The corner with all the mouth came up for a tackle; I hit a quick step back and made him miss. He managed to grab a hold of my leg so I muffed his head into the ground making his facemask meet the grass. It was almost like he threw his body at me. PJ and Chris were helpful by blocking their butts off. After I grabbed the ball and made a move, I saw all daylight. I ran eight yards and saw a linebacker flying my direction to cut me off for an easy tackle, I cut back making him miss. I cut back again creating extra space, making another man miss.

I became one –on- one with a corner from the other side of the field. I planted my foot hard in the grass, he went for it but tried to regain his balance, so I planted again and made him fall awkwardly. I left Brook Dale in my dust.

My teammates cheered me on as I jogged back.

"Clutch!!!!!"

"Good work Clutch!"

"That man Clutch!"

Our defense did just what I thought they were going to do, they completely murdered Brook Dale offense. They made at least seven yards after running at least 20 plays.

Travis is actually a really good cornerback, he has the potential to be a starter. I'm rooting for him, really, as long as he stops fooling around with me because I'm not somebody to toy with. I might end up hurting him after getting fed up.

Coach Louie kept feeding me the rock on offense. After my first score, I scored again about four more times. Bertron ran for two touch downs and threw at least six through the air. After a while Louie made the starting group sit out and watch. I tried to get in on defense and play safety but Louie wasn't going to let that happen. We watched our second team offense and defense put up numbers as well. That was the scary part about our team, our first and second groups are very good.

"Line up on the fifty," both coaches yelled.

We shook hands with Brook Dale. They didn't really want to shake our hands because of the way we destroyed them, although most of their players did show some respect. A few of the guys even complimented me.

"Good job number one."

"Good job one."

Their head coach shook my hand genuinely as he put his other hand around my shoulder pads.

"Good job one, you're a hell of a player, wish you guys the best of luck this season."

"Thanks Coach, you too," I replied as I jogged over into our end zone where my other teammates were.

Coach Louie stepped up, "Tremendous! I really liked what I've seen out on that field today. Clap it up guys!"

As we clapped, he talked more about us playing hard and keeping our composure when Brook Dale barked at us. I can tell he doesn't want us to get too comfortable.

"It's Friday, be safe over the weekend, try to eat healthy, drink lots of water, and rest," Coach Louie said. "See you boys Monday at 2:00, break us out Clutch."

I cleared my throat a little so I could yell loud enough for everyone to hear me, "Hard work, dedication on three, one, two, three."

"HARDWORK-DEDICATION!!!!" We shouted and ran for the locker room.

Before running off, Coach Louie called me over.

"Clutch good job out there today bud," Louie said.

"Thanks Coach."

"I want you to rest up and remain focused all weekend, meaning stay off your feet," Louie said.

"Yes Coach," I replied.

He smacked my shoulder pads dimly.

After getting undressed it was around 7:45 so I knew I had to get home to Dee Dee. I walked home with Bertron and Mark and we talked and laughed about the scrimmage the whole way home. Jerry and his gang were standing on the outside of a local corner store.

"Yooooo yooo!" Jerry said.

We all stopped and looked.

"Y'all wanna make some extra money?" Jerry asked.

"Sure!" Mark said.

I thought about the extra money we can use at home, but then I thought about the consequences from accepting money from a guy like Jerry. I don't trust that guy, not one bit.

"Nahh man we good Bro," I said. "Let's go."

I walked off, Bertron followed but Mark hesitated. Bertron called him and he caught up to us.

"What is y'all doing man, y'all tweaking. Y'all missing out on an opportunity to get money!"

I stopped and grabbed him by his shirt aggressively.

"That's just an opportunity to get your dumb ass killed Bro, use your tiny ass brain dude," I warned him. "Do you wanna play ball in school, or be on the street making money risking your life, stupid? Huh? Make up your mind right now."

He slapped my hands down.

"I wanna do both!"

At this moment I just wanted to slap the shit out of this dude but Bertron got between us.

"Yo chill!"

"I need the money, you need the money, stop acting like we live a rich lifestyle," Mark said.

"Go! Go be on the streets and let your life blow right passed you!" I screamed at him.

He looked down the block at Jerry and the rest of them.

"I guess I will then," Mark said as he walked away from us toward Jerry and his dirty friends.

Bertron and I walked home.

"Iight man be safe," Bertron said.

"Iight Bruh you too," I said waving to him.

I made it home and ran upstairs anxious for a shower. Mark was on my mind the whole way, we've been best friends since seventh grade recess and he's just risking it all for a few bucks.

"Rajon!!" Dee Dee tackled me. "Ugh you smell like outside," she said.

"That's the smell of true, hard work little one. You better take notes," I explained while tickling her. "Have you been practicing on your handles?"

"Yes," she said as she jumped out of my arms and pretends to dribble a ball through her legs. "Some man named Louie called to make sure you were in the house."

"That's my coach," I told her. "Did Mom leave any money for food?"

"No she left you a note on the refrigerator."

I went in the kitchen and took the note down and read:

> *A bill was passed due and it was mandatory that I pay it in order to keep the lights on. Please do what you can to make things work. See you soon. Love, Mom.*

At that very moment I thought about that money Jerry offered, then I got upset with myself for thinking that stupid. I had no choice but to look around the kitchen for food. Our refrigerator was old and empty and the cabinet doors in the kitchen were ancient and raggedy. We were starving so I called her dad to see if he could bring by some grocery money. He claimed he was five minutes away, but we waited three hours for him.

I decided to toast stale bread from last month, so we ate warm bread and shared sink water. That night I also found out something about life, if you want something done, you'll have to do it yourself, plain and simple. That became my newest motto.

The next morning I was hoping to see Mom. She usually comes home around one on Saturdays. She works two jobs Monday through Friday, every week from 12 a.m. to 12 p.m. including both jobs. The next morning I was up early looking over my playbook. I love the new plays Coach Louie installed because it looks like I'll be getting the ball all season, so that means scholarships are on the way.

This is my last season so that means I have to be dominant. Great is not good enough anymore. If you want to make it to the top without a doubt, you have to be dominant. I live in a place where people don't really make it where I'm from. Just being able to attend college would truly be a blessing. Dee Dee woke up later than I did. I decided to take her to a playground basketball court to work on her handles and shooting form.

I called Bertron to see if he wanted to come along. I also asked him to bring Dee Dee and myself something to snack on since there wasn't anything to look forward to in this house.

The court was empty, but that's the way I like it because it gives me the space I need to help Dee Dee on her game. I told Dee Dee to stretch as I took a couple shots waiting for Bertron to show up. We started out working on her left hand dribble. I made her drive to the rim while I pressured her waist with my right hand. She's good and I have no clue how she got so quick. Her shot is nice and her handles get better every time I see her on the court.

Meanwhile, Bertron showed up with a plastic bag.

"Good looking out man, we're starving," I said.

"I know how you feel man," said Bertron.

He already knew Dee Dee and I haven't eaten, because he brought two sandwiches, chips, fruit roll ups, and a juice box. Dee Dee ate her food while bouncing the ball and Bertron and I sat on the bench.

"Have you talked to Mark since last night?" Bertron asked.

"Nah, I called him but his grandma said he wasn't in. I hope he doesn't get himself into trouble," I said.

"True," Bertron said.

After another hour of talking and training Dee Dee, we started to wrap it up and walk home. I bounced the ball walking back and I had seen Corbin on the way. Corbin was the best basketball player in West Wood

High last year. He had colleges lined up at his doorstep, although his grades weren't pleasant. I heard he got this trashy girl pregnant and dropped out after his basketball season his senior year. That's sad if you ask me. That's why I just stay focused and don't let the distractions get to me. There isn't a girl in this world that will ever knock me off my game and make me unfocused. My ambition is too strong for that.

I broke up with girls in my past just because they were starting to affect my grind on the field. I remember this one girl told me it was either football or me.

I laughed in her face and told her to take care. I look at it like this, if you're not pushing me to help me succeed then I don't need you. Point- blank period. There's no way around that.

Bertron made a right once we got to the corner after walking four blocks down. Dee Dee and I arrived home after walking for five more minutes. Suddenly we got upstairs and Mom was on the couch lying restless. There were bags on the table, so I'm guessing she picked up a few things for the house.

"Mom!!!" Dee Dee rushed to her eagerly and hugged her.

I can tell she was beyond exhausted. I went over and gave her a hug as she hugged me and kissed my forehead.

"I see you guys have been keeping each other busy,"

Mom said.

"Yeah pretty much, we worked on her shooting and foot work today down at the court."

"You know that area is not safe," Mom said.

"Mom when she's with me, she's always safe, this city is mine," I told her.

Mom laughed, I was just enjoying the moment of seeing her. I felt so grateful even though she was drowsy.

"How's football?" Mom asked.

I was more than pleased to tell her everything.

"Football has been going great; I don't think Google would even tell you how to guard me," I said while beating on my chest tenderly.

"That's what I want to hear Son."

Mom's eyes got lower by the minute.

    I knew she needed to rest so I kissed her cheek and walked in the kitchen to put away the food she brought home. About an hour later an alarm clock went off. Mom hopped up and grabbed a black bag with two long straps swiftly. My mood became gloomy because I already knew what that meant, it was 4:00 and she had to get back to her part- time job.

    Mom kissed Dee Dee and myself then went for

the door. I spent the rest of that evening thinking about the times Mom and I shared. I managed to fall asleep a little while later until the sound of our house phone woke me up. It was Coach Louie, he told me he had good news and he wanted to stop by to share it with my mom and me. I told him my mom was at work but I'm still free to listen to anything that's good news.

Coach knocked on my door 10 minutes later. I opened it and invited him in for a seat. Dee Dee stuck her head around the corner to see who was at the door.

"Talk to me Coach," I said as I sat down.

"Where is Mark? And why hasn't he been in practice lately?" Coach asked as he sat down.

I wanted to tell him the truth, but I didn't want him to cut Mark from the team.

"I think he's been real sick," I said, trying not to make eye contact with him. For some reason he can always tell when I'm lying.

"Before coming over I was on the phone with a few coaches from a few different schools and they all are very interested in you, Son."

My eyes were glued on Coach. I didn't even want to blink.

"Keep talking to me," I said as I folded my hands with my forearms resting on my knees.

"Kentucky, Oregon, Ohio State, LSU, and Maryland

will be scouting you throughout the season. It will be up to you to keep your grades up and play with a passion week after week from here on out."

I immediately started to smirk. I was so geeked but I kept a productive composure.

"I'm very pleased Coach, I will not let my family or the team down, and I mean that."

"Just don't let yourself down, Son," Coach Louie said as he put his rough hands on my shoulder. "I have faith in you to stay consistent and motivated."

"You have my word Coach," I said.

We talked more for about two whole hours until Louie looked at his watch.

"I didn't notice how late it had gotten," Louie said as he got up and went for the door.

He had a hard time trying to open it. I stood there for a second watching him wrestle with the door knob.

"It's kind of an old door Coach," I said as I opened it for him.

"I'm counting on you Clutch," he said as he turned to me before leaving.

"Indeed Coach."

I closed the door and wanted to do a back flip. I was so happy, I raced for the room to give Dee Dee the good news.

"Don't leave us, please we need you Rajon!!" Dee Dee cried.

I'm guessing she heard my coach name the far away colleges that are scouting me. Her crying destroyed my whole mood, I felt bad at the moment. I grabbed her and laid her head on my chest.

"Listen Dee Dee, I'm not going nowhere any time soon. After high school football I have to go off to college and play at the next level to make you and Mom proud," I said as I hugged her firmly. "Don't you want to see your big brother on TV making touchdowns?" I asked her as I wiped the tears from her eyes.

She shook her head up and down. I knew she was still sad though. I absolutely hate when Dee Dee cries, as her big brother I just cannot take it.

The next morning I woke up thinking about the conversation Coach Louie and I had. I was anxious to share the news with Mom just to see how she felt. It became bittersweet, really, thinking about Dee Dee not wanting me to leave. I started doing my pushups in the mirror in our room, I did five sets of 20 and my arms were tight after my slight workout. I blew my morning kiss to God then decided to get in the shower.

I knew I had practice the next day so I tried to burn as much time as I could by taking naps, watching TV, and mainly looking over plays. Monday morning I was up and ready for action. I called Bertron to throw me some passes before practice. We walked up to the field and got a nice workout in for about three hours. I went home just to rest for a quick minute and regain energy. I kissed Dee Dee on the forehead and left for the door.

Bertron and I met back up at his corner and got to practice 20 minutes early. We talked and joked around for a minute until it was time to get dressed. One thing about me is I can be a class clown and crack jokes all day, but when I lace up my cleats and hit the gridiron, there's nothing funny about that.

Suddenly Coach Louie walked in and called me into his office. I felt important every time I stepped foot through that door. He had so many newspaper articles, achievements, awards, pictures, hanging up on the wall. I noticed there were even pictures of me on the wall as I arrived at his door.

"Have a seat Clutch," he said as he leaned back in his black leather chair.

There was a Best Buy bag sitting on his desk. He grabbed it and threw it on my lap.

"Check it out," Coach said.

I looked in it and it was a pair of brand new Beats headphones. My heart started racing fast, I had seen a commercial last week of the same ones I was holding in my hands.

"These are nice Coach," I said as I examined them with

my eyes.

"Those are yours Clutch," Louie said.

I stood up quickly. "Nah Coach I can't take these from you," I said as I put them back in the bag and sat them down.

"Of course you can, you've earned them," Coach said.

I didn't know what Coach wanted from me. I hope he wasn't expecting me to ever pay for them unless I made it pro, but that's years from now.

"I want you to use these to stay focused and get in the zone before any event we have," Coach said.

In my eyes, Coach wanted me to have the headphones to get in the zone instead of laughing around in the locker room before a practice or game. Coach Louie was scaring me, but I took the headphones and got dressed for practice. I put the plastic bag in my book bag before anyone saw it my hand.

Practice was very intense as always, we ran plays after plays. Coach Louie made us go against the second defense group. In my eyes you shouldn't take them light because there are a lot of kids that want to prove themselves and earn a starting position. At that moment I took my own advice and completely destroyed those guys. I have no mercy for any defender, no matter if you are good or not. You can be my teammate, best friend, brother, uncle, or even my teacher, but if you step in front of me, attempting to

46

guard me, you're going to get this work!

      I think it's very disrespectful for anyone to step in front of me as a defender. I try my best to insult your skill, expose the weakness of your ankles, test your ability, disparage your confidence, and just disregard you as a person. I have no clue where the anger in me comes from, but I like it and it will be released every time I strap up my helmet. I will not stop until my mom stops working. There's a lion in me, he's hungry, he makes me hungrier, together, we are greedy.

Second Quarter

Later on after practice that night I laid down thinking about my life. I have a lot on my mind, I was deep into my thoughts. I think about my future every single day. I want to see billions, ASAP! My grandma once told me before she died to be somebody. She told me to make something good out my life, and to not be in the streets with my pants hanging low like I have no home training. I miss her more than anything, she left a mark on my heart. When life gets too hard I just want to be with her, but after thinking to myself, I would let Mom and Dee Dee down. So I have to catch my dreams before I leave this earth. Life is not easy for anyone, so I must make the best out of mine daily.

The moment I decided to close my eyes, I heard the loudest gun shots outside of my window, they sounded like they were right downstairs from my building. Some nights there are so many gunshots, it sounds like Iraq. That's the main reason why people call the city of Illinois "Chi-raq." I decided to call Mark just to check on him. His grandma said he wasn't home. I tried my best not to worry after hearing that. I just don't want to lose my right hand man to these streets. I suddenly started getting sleepy, so I blew a kiss to God and dozed off.

The next morning the house phone rang early. It was West Wood High calling to remind and inform everyone that school starts back up in less than two weeks. The feeling was bittersweet. The only good part of school being so close was going into my senior season. I feel closer to my dreams as these long days go passed. My whole entire summer was spent on the football field, nowhere else but the gridiron. I just don't know what real fun is. I mean, I have lots of fun on the field and I feel like that's all the fun I need, I'm just talking about other excitement. I guess that's later in my future after Mom stops working.

Eight days went by and it's the same routine every day of the week: early morning grind, struggle with food, catching 200 balls, running routes, making people fall in practice, making plays, training Dee Dee on the court, hoping to see Mom, and just counting my blessings day by day as life goes on because life never stops for anyone.

Dee Dee's dad came by to drop off a few things for her for school. That was a shocking surprise that he knew it was even time for school. I just hate it when he feels like he gave her the world just because he came by to give her $80.00, school supplies, and some outfits. How big of a drug dealer is he? He should be able to do that every other day or week.

I was hoping to see Mom today. She would leave a note any time she stopped by when we were asleep. I just don't understand why she works so much. I mean, I get it that it's only her taking care of us and bills pile up, but damn, I just really miss her and if that's the case, I can get a part-time job when school starts after my football season. I just want to spend a full day with her.

I get mad when I see someone complain about their parents. It makes them look very unappreciative. No matter how much your parents make you upset, be thankful that they are even there to yell at you. I wish my mom was here yelling at me. That's the sad part about teens, they don't understand that once you start to appreciate the little things about life and everything you have, they will have a brand new outlook on life itself.

It was three days before school and I wasn't prepared. I had the same old clothes from sophomore and junior year. I always made it work though, really since I'm an athlete, I prefer to dress like one. We can get away with a lot, only if you're good though. That means shorts, gym shoes, and a football shirt. Mom never had enough money to get me up- to- date clothes like the new Dri-fit Nike and other popular brands. It's cool though, I never trip. I don't need all the designer jeans and clothing to fit in.

It's practice time and it is a very beautiful day today to be doing so. The sun is out, birds are singing, and you can hear the Chicago traffic blocks away. It even smells like football, only football players can relate to that. Sometimes you can even hear the shooting from blocks away. The gun shots never stop us from practicing, every time it happens, everyone pauses for a quick moment and hope it's no one that they knew, and then get right back to work.

Today is our last day of summer camp practice before the first day of school. I'd like to finish off the summer on a good note, check that, a great note.

Practice started right on time. Coach had us doing one - on -ones in the start of practice today. I have a feeling Coach has a lot of intense things planned today, if so, then we're on the exact same page. I just love doing one- on –ones, I feel like it's a drill just to make me look good as the receiver.

Here you have a receiver versus a corner with no help over the top. It's every man for himself during a one –on- one situation. I stepped to the line waiting for a corner to step up. Those corners knew to think twice before facing me. I mean, I wouldn't even want to face myself if I was cloned as a corner. I like to expose with no mercy. Travis popped out the defense line clapping his hands together like he was Superman or something, I smirked.

I was hoping he would step up, little does he know, I wanted him more than he wanted me. The defensive players cheered Travis on which made me a little mad, so now I have to expose his ass even more and shut everybody up. I strapped up my gloves tight and chewed down on my mouthpiece fiercely.

"You not catching the ball," Travis said as he lined up in front of me.

I didn't want to say anything back because I had something special planned for him. It feels good letting your game speak for you, talk is cheap.

The actions that I make are way louder than anything I will ever say to this confused kid. I was in my ready position looking at BJ to snap the ball. I stared at Travis wanting him to feel like he was looking in the eyes of a hungry, blood thirsty lion in the dark, cold, windy nights of Africa. He stared back in my eyes, sweat dripping down his forehead between his eyes. I don't think he even wanted to guard me; I respect him for attempting though. I want to break this guy apart. He must really think I'm a joke or something, like I just have white and red paint on my face.

The ball snapped, Travis went for the jam as always, silly rabbit. I smacked his hands away and went for a fade route and he followed me in my trail. I wanted to confuse his eyes if they're watching my hips. I moved as swiftly as I could and I left him two yards behind me. He held onto my practice jersey and I slowed down to let him catch up for a moment. I broke down as quickly as I could, stopping for a hitch route leaving him in the opposite direction.

BJ threw a bullet, I grabbed it, and turned up field for a light jog. Travis seemed embarrassed as he was getting up off the ground when I passed him. He gave me a clear cheap shot out of nowhere. Boom! I stumbled, trying my best to keep myself from falling. At this moment I was ready to beat his ass, there's nothing else he had to say or do to me. I ran towards him ready to swing on my guards. BJ and three of our linemen grabbed me as quick as they could. I was beyond heated, that was so weak of him to do something like that.

Coach Louie grabbed Travis almost killing him.

He yelled at him like he was a dog and made him run laps around the whole football field for the rest of practice. I still wanted a piece of that weak punk, I don't care how many laps he does. I was thinking about getting him in the locker room but I changed my mind after I calmed down. I want to be a humble player, but it's just guys like him that press the wrong buttons.

After running routes, Coach Louie had us take a knee so all the coaches could talk to us. I can tell he was still mad about what Travis did, he still had him jogging around the field as they talked. Coach talked about staying focused and keeping our grades up throughout the season. I knew what he meant, he was basically saying don't get distracted from all the girls and high school drama. He didn't have to worry about me.

I haven't had a girlfriend since my freshman year. She was perfect and she kept me focused on school and was very supportive, but it was too good to be true. One day she flipped on me by saying she wanted to run our relationship and I had no choice but to end it there. I kind of miss her, but she messed up with me though. Those girls are way too easy at Westwood, they just throw themselves at me and expect me to date them. Girls like that are called "thots" around here.

Girls are my least main focus until I'm ready to get married… Maybe. When I look at a girl, she has to be perfect enough to be my wife. I would never, ever be affiliated with a girl that I can't see becoming my future wife. Not to be on the cocky side, but there has never been a girl I couldn't get. Every girl I ever wanted, I've gotten. Just like a ball traveling through the air, it's mine, just that easy!

Coach told me to meet him in his office, I'm tired of meeting this man in his office. He needs to meet me in my locker room for a change. After I got dressed, I walked in and stood at the door. The other coaches were just leaving. They gave me pats on the shoulder as they walked passed then Louie asked me to close the door.

"Clutch, how ya feeling buddy?" Coach asked.

"I'm great Coach," I said as I sat in the chair across from his desk.

He picked up a nice sized black duffle bag and sat it on his desk. It looked heavy.

"Take a look inside," Coach Louie said.

In the bag there were so many different kinds of hoodies and sweat pants. I saw West Wood football, Oklahoma football, Ohio State football, and so much more clothing to choose from. The bag was filled with clothes and school supplies. At that moment I felt poor.

"Coach what do you want from me?" I asked in an indigently way.

"I want you to be successful Clutch!!" Coach said as he stared at me.

"Nah man, I'm gonna be successful without a doubt," I said as I walked out.

I didn't even know how to feel. Coach Louie just wanted to help, but what does he even know about me besides football? Mom is doing a good enough job with me. I'm good, I don't want all the extra help from Coach Louie. Maybe I'm upset because Coach Louie does all the things that I wish my father was here to do for me. I walked straight home by myself, I didn't even bother to wait on anyone else. I just needed to clear my head of all thoughts.

The night was still young after practice. When I got home, I got right in the shower then just laid in the bed thinking about what happened on the field with Travis and then I thought about that black bag. I felt dumb for not taking it. I felt like Coach just wants me to fully focus on football and not have anything else to worry about. Dee Dee knew something was wrong with me, she knows me best. I still acted like everything was okay though. I managed to take a nap even though I wasn't that sleepy. I woke up around 10:37 when I heard a knock on the door.

Dee Dee was asleep on the couch in the living room. I opened it hoping it was Mark. It was Coach Louie standing there at my doorstep holding that same black duffle bag. He never said a word when he put it in my arms and walked away.

"Thanks Coach," I said before slamming the door shut.

I felt like he read my mind. I took the bag into my room and dumped everything on my old stained mattress. It had 12 different hoodies and shirts, 10 pairs of shorts and sweat pants, cargo, and athletic type, Nike socks, school supplies, and even money. I just stood there in shock. It felt like Christmas, a Christmas I never had before, and a birthday that finally came. I'm speechless. More importantly, I felt like I was ready for school now. I put all the items back in the bag and left out what I was wearing on the first day of school.

The money rested in a thick, yellow envelope. I counted it over and over again. Dee Dee woke up and we ran to the corner store nearby to grab a few items. I bought deodorant, soap, Gatorade, tooth paste, and my favorite TV dinners.

"Where did you get money?" Dee Dee asked.

"From a good friend," I said to her.

"Are you doing the things my dad is doing?" She asked me.

"Dee Dee don't be stupid, I will never do anything that crazy. Understand?" I said as I put all the items on the counter.

"Understood," she said as she put her items up there too.

I don't like the fact that she knows her dad sells

drugs. There are just some things that she shouldn't know about. Our total was $48.63, Dee Dee gave me 25 dollars that her dad gave her, and I paid the rest.

When we got in the house, I put the food and drinks away and started eating. Afterwards Dee Dee and I watched a little TV. I sat there looking through my playbook most of the time. Coach Louie just installed new signals and I know he expects me to have it down to a science.

The next morning I woke up bright and early feeling good. I've questioned myself and wondered why I don't like to sleep a lot, I came up with a conclusion that I'm not where I want to be in life so my hunger keeps me on the move. I never get to sleep for a long period of time, anyway. I wake up every morning around 6:30 just to thank God for giving me another day to chase my dreams.

I called PJ about six times, I knew he was still sleeping. When he finally answered we got on the field for about two hours for a morning workout. We had two days to rest so he wasn't really feeling the whole workout thing, as for me, I hated resting. How much rest does a teenager need? I'm young, I can rest when Mom stops working. Right now it's time to make things happen. Grind now, sleep later, I have always told myself and others: you can feel sore tomorrow, or you can feel sorry tomorrow. It's your choice to decide today at this very moment.

It's impossible to dream big and sleep a lot.

You have to work on making your dream come true by being focused and being comfortable with being uncomfortable. If you are someone who want everything to come easy then you need to readjust your comfort zone. How hard you work now determines how much you will get paid in the future. There are no secrets to success, it's nothing about success that is not allowed for you to know and fully understand.

    The day before school came quickly. I packed my gym bag with a few notebooks, pens, and my practice gear. Later on in the day I was chilling looking over plays again. Coach Louie called me to make sure I was ready for my first day of senior year, he was talking about how proud he was of me. By the time we got off the phone I was ready for bed. I tried going to sleep but I kept getting up to look at the clothes I'm wearing tomorrow to school. Everything is new. I've never went to school ever in my life with new socks, clothes, and other items, everything has always been used. I was geeked, I can't wait until tomorrow. I truly hope that I enjoy my senior year, I have a very strong feeling that I will.

    I came into Westwood freshman year thinking everything was a joke and that mindset caught up to me as the years went by. I was behind on credits for a while, struggling to catch up. High school isn't hard or easy, it's what you make of it. The work you get builds on what you learned in middle school, giving you a more advanced knowledge of different academic subjects. The smartest thing you can do once you get to high school is play sports. Playing sports will make high school way better than what it already is.

Halftime

    Rest in peace summer break, it's now Monday morning and it's time for school. I feel so blessed to be in the position that I'm in today. I made it all the way to my last year in high school without getting killed or dropping out like the rest. I could have been a drug dealer or somebody's pimp but I chose to catch passes, run routes, and go down the right path to get closer to my dreams.

    I know my grandma is proud of me, I just know she is. I can just imagine her beautiful smile and her telling me how much of a great young man I've became over the past few years, the feeling is heartwarming. I'm very proud of myself for making it this far. I had lots of speed bumps and dark tunnels on this long journey, although my journey has just begun. There have been so many days when I wanted to just give up on life and school. Sometimes I used to ask God why He even brought me into this world. Then I ask myself how I could even question God. I feel like I wasn't made for school.

    I'm not much of a book smart person or a good test taker. I hate putting my full name on tests preparing myself to make a fool out of myself, most of the time I actually try my best. I just don't like sitting in classrooms waiting to not know the answer to a question my teacher will ask me. The annoying part about that situation is: half of the time the teacher will know I don't know the answer but still decides to ask me out loud in front of the class to try to embarrass me. Then teachers wonder why students skip class so much. I'm just gifted with knowledge about life and success. I just know how to do things in order to make it out. I'm more street smart than book smart.

I want to be on the honor roll list and rank top 10 in my class but school is just not for me. I'm just determined to be wealthy and happy with my mother and Dee Dee by my side. I just want to graduate on time and move on, that's all.

I decided to get ready for school after doing my daily morning push-ups, I need to get bigger and stronger. Some days I keep count, other days I do as many as I can until my arms start shaking really bad. Class starts at 8:20, and it's 7:00 on the dot. I was ready and out the door around 7:48. Dee Dee goes to school right around the corner from West Wood, she walks to and from school every day with her classmates. This proves she's very responsible for her age. Everyone around also knows she belongs to me so there should not be any problems.

Bells ringing, switching classes, taking notes, spreading rumors, and asking to borrow someone's pen or pencil is what high school is all about. I'm very eager to start off my senior year with a successful season and acceptable grades. I woke up in a productive mood. It's my first day of senior year.

Walking through the halls felt good, I'm kind of excited but I notice there was no sign of Mark yet. I had my football summer camp shirt on with my shorts to match and my favorite Nike air max. I shook hands and bumped fists with all the guys I haven't seen all summer and hugged lots of girls that claimed they missed me over the break. The love I was receiving was real, reuniting with everyone made the school day go by quickly.

I like most of my classes except Algebra 2. I hate any type of math with a passion. I question myself, *why in the hell do we need to find X? X is obviously lost so there's no need to look for a letter that we won't find in the lost and found box.* I know how to count money so all the extra math questions will not do me any justice, but that's just my opinion.

Three of my teachers seem more focused on my football season than anything else which is great, so I'll be expecting a 100% in those classes for sure just from playing a good game. In lunch all of the football players sat at the same table. Our cheerleaders sit with us some days, other days they sit at a table near us. We talked and cracked jokes the whole entire time, catching up with each other. No matter how much I joke and laugh, I'm always game ready. I'm eager to win. I can tell that everyone wanted to be around us just from how good we are as a team. I had a class with a few of the guys on the team: BJ, PJ, and Daniel.

After my last period class I hung out at my locker for a little bit. After a while I grabbed my bag and headed to practice.

I walked through the building heading to our main gym where all the athletes go after school before practice. There you have us, who are the football players, next you have our cheer leaders. A lot of them have a crush on me, even the ones with boyfriends, but that's none of my business. I don't pay those stuck up girls any mind though. Then you have our volleyball players. I like a few of them, Deanna Stewart is my main crush on that team. She's about 5'2," very athletic, brown eyes, and black hair and she gives me the chills when I see her in her tight spandex bottoms. I heard she likes me but I'm not focused on relationships at the moment. Football is my girlfriend right now unless I find someone who is qualified and plays hard to get. I see the most beautiful girls everyday all over the school, but none of them impress me enough to give any of them a chance.

Coach Louie walked in the gym. The players who saw him first sprinted to the locker room to get dressed. I didn't see him because I was too busy talking to Deanna over by the bleachers.

"Clutch!!" Louie yelled.

My eyes got big instantly just from hearing the sound of his voice

"Yes Coach," I replied as my stomach dropped.

"Do you wanna make plays or get caught up what you doing now?" Coach asked me.

I felt so embarrassed. He could've asked me something like that in private or when we got on the practice field.

"Make plays Coach."

I had no other choice but to just grab my gym bag and go get dressed.

I had a feeling Coach was mad at me for talking to Deanna instead of being in the locker room dressed for practice. Coach came into our locker room as we all got dressed. Boom!! Boom!! Boom!! Coach Louie smacked on the locker with his thick, brown clip board.

"From now on I want all of you in this God damn locker room dressed and ready to go before practice, if anyone has a problem with that you can return all your equipment now and get your ass out this building," Louie said.

"Yes Coach," we all replied back as a team.

I was on my way to the practice field for stretching when I suddenly bumped a girl on the way, she's a girl I've never seen before here at West Wood. I think she was mixed or something, she had to be.

"Excuse me, I'm sorry," I said as I gazed into her eyes.

"It's ok," she replied as she walked off.

At that moment I was hoping Coach Louie didn't see me, but if he did then I'll suffer the consequences later because she's all that!

"Wait are you new here?" I asked her as I followed her and looked back at the door for any sign of Louie.

"No, I've been here as long as you Rajon," she said.

"What's your name?" I asked her.

Before she could even reply Coach Louie walked out with the other coaches, my heart started to beat fast.

"Catch you later," I said to the girl as I put on my helmet and jogged onto the field.

  This girl was on my mind during stretches. She's the only girl in the school that never tried to get my attention, I can tell she was something special. After I strapped up my helmet I was strictly football focused. Coach called me over and gave me a lecture about being and staying focused. The first game is this Friday night and we play South Wood in our house. There will be cameras, scouts, and fans all over the place. Our stadium will be filled from the bleachers to the sidelines.

  Coach had us doing hitting drills in the start of practice to get us ready for South Wood. I'm pretty sure their head coach is familiar with me so he will attempt to stop me on each and every play. Last season I scored on their defense all game long for four quarters straight. I played so well to the point their head coach came up to me after the game and offered to come play for him, I think he was even willing to pay.

  I wouldn't leave West Wood; I'll always be a

Lion at heart. Around where we stay, after middle school you either end up attending West Wood or South Wood. We are all familiar with each other so this game is very important to both schools. The whole community discusses who's going win every year. To make a bet on the game, you'll have to go in any local barbershop in the area.

Coach had us working hard all week until Thursday. I felt like we were going to be too sore for the game Friday if we didn't slow down a little, but only a little.

When I got to school, I kind of searched for that mixed girl I ran into Monday before practice. She was nowhere to be found, and I felt like a stalker so I stopped. Days into school weren't bad at all.

Everyone is just anxious for our first home game, West Wood has pride. Thursday came quicker than a taxi cab in New York City. I already had butterflies in my stomach for the game. We did a walk through and watched film on South Wood from last season. They have some pretty good athletes. I'm pretty good friends with most of their best players. The best part about being a great athlete is we all read about each other in the *Sun-Times*.

After film, Coach gave us our game jerseys to wear for the next day in school. We have five different uniforms. Home games, we wear our black and gold jerseys with grey pants. A lot of the football players give their girlfriend their away jersey to wear around

66

the school on game day. I don't have a girlfriend so I give my jersey to Dee Dee to wear to the game. As Louie passed out jerseys I had seen number three hanging up, that's Mark's jersey. My mood was erupted at that exact moment, Mark doesn't even come to school anymore. I can't worry about him too much though. I have to focus my mind on more important things. I will not allow myself to babysit someone who is around the same age as I am.

      After practice Thursday, Coach gave me a black plastic bag. I was so anxious to see what was in it. When I got home I dumped the bag on my bed. Four pairs of Nike football gloves, Nike bands, black Nike socks and more game day accessories. Later that night I hung up my jersey before going to sleep. I put my jersey at the end of Dee Dee's bed then kissed her on the forehead.

      Friday morning felt like payday. The moment I opened my eyes, I smiled and started to beat on my chest. It's GAME DAY BABY!!!! I felt so emotional and charged up, it's finally time to put it all on the field. After all the hard work, long, hot practices, and pain, it's finally here! My question of the day is, who's going to stop number one!?

      I listened to some rap music and got dressed. I had a note on my jersey from Mom which meant she stopped home just to write me a note for my first game of the season. I knew she wouldn't forget, but I really wish she could make it. After reading my note from Mom, I became anxious. I'm pissed off for greatness. I dare for someone to attempt to stop me tonight. I'm focused! I kissed Dee Dee on the forehead and walked out.

I walked to school wearing my jersey proudly. My headphones were up loud but my loud music didn't stop my thoughts from going through my head. People on the block patted me on the shoulder as I walked passed for good luck I guess. I didn't say a word, I was thinking about tonight and everything I'm going to do.

During school I had my headphones on for most of the day and I didn't smile at all in school. My teachers and everyone else wished me luck and kept all conversations short, they knew I was game focused. From the lunch ladies to the janitors, everyone in West Wood knew I was in my zone. Game time came around fast ending the school day. During my last class, I could not sit still. I felt like a lion standing on top of a mountain in the jungle roaring, letting everyone know it was lunch time.

An hour before the game we prayed in the locker room then stretched on our practice field. Coach Louie gave us a long speech. I felt everything he was saying but I was just ready to play ball. We showed up on our game field five minutes later.

South Wood was already on the field warming up. It was a full house of course, it looked like the whole neighborhood came out to watch because there weren't any empty seats. Scouts were lined up at the top of the bleachers, photographers and sports journalists were tuned into the game as well. Our school band was beating the drums so hard it made my blood rush. We all stood behind a black gate separating us from the field waiting for it to open for an interest. We call it the Lions' Den. Inside it, we have two thermal foggers that shoot out lots of smoke before we run off onto the field, giving it an eerie effect and showing fans we mean business.

"Give it up for your West Wood High Lions!!!" The announcer exclaimed.

We rushed onto the field as the crowd went wild. Our game day theme song was loud, it was so loud I couldn't even hear myself think. I jogged and held up one finger, that's just letting everyone know to watch number one, they better know. The clock read 5:34 which means it's time for the National Anthem. I took off my helmet and gave it to our trainer.

Light drops of rain started to landed on my face as I looked into the sky. I pulled my headband over my face onto my mouth trying to keep the rain out of my face. At that point I felt a connection with God. After the Anthem the rain all of a sudden stopped. I think it was God's way of cleaning the field and allowing me to own every inch of this gridiron. The referees called for the captains who were BJ, PJ, our middle linebacker named Trey, and myself. We then walked over to the middle of the field.

South Wood quarterback, running back, and two defensive players walked up, they were my homies from middle school. We won the coin toss and asked to receive the ball first. At that moment I just knew it was game time. Coach Louie sent our kick return group out on the field. Mark used to be back there deep as our return man, but now it's PJ's time to shine. We huddled on the sideline, Louie called two plays. Spread twins X quick, and strong right, fake 17 post fade double smack gridiron.

I blew a kiss to my grandma who watches over me from heaven, and then I looked over where Dee Dee always sit and blew her a kiss as well. She was looking directly at me and she caught it with both hands. The last and final kiss I blew was to God. I asked God to bring the lion out of me. I'm an ambitious athlete and an ambitious lion sleeps inside of me, he comes out and attacks the moment I get competitive. PJ returned the kick for 23 yards, which is not bad. Offense went out and we got set soon as the whistle blew to start this show we're about to put on.

All eyes are on us. The West Wood Lions are running the show now. The snap count was on ready, I'm lined up on the left side of the field. The defense wasn't all the way set.

"Ready!!" BJ screamed.

I went two steps up and two steps back towards the ball, I grabbed it and instantly shot up field using all of my blocking support. A corner dived at my feet, I jumped over him with ease, and ran down the sideline pointing towards the end zone. I slowed down the moment I crossed the goal line.

"Touchdown! Number one Rajon Clutch Rodgers! Seventy seven- yard pass from number 12 Brendon Jones for a West Wood Lion Touchdown!" The announcer shouted.

      The crowd went completely nuts and stood for a standing ovation. I took one knee and blew a kiss to Grandma. A couple of my teammates rushed to me and they all smacked my shoulder pads and helmet. Louie was fired up, he kept us on the field for the two- point conversion. He called a play to Daniel, he ran right up the middle trucking defenders for two points. After kick-off our defense was even more fired up. South Wood managed to get to mid- field before having to punt the ball.

The ball was kicked pretty well so we took over at the 20-yard line. Louie signaled a pass play from the sideline. I had a fade route and the free safety had an eye on me.

"Watch number one! Watch number one!" He warned.

      My corner started creeping up on me like he was going for the jam at the line. He's number eight on South Wood and he's pretty good I heard. I slowly started to position my hands to get ready for any move he made. The ball was snapped, I positioned my whole body to go in, then I went to the outside smacking his hands to the inside of me. I was striding down the field with my corner about six yards behind. The safety spotted me quickly as the ball traveled my way. My eyes got big, I caught the ball as I stumbled.

I fell down at the five- yard line reaching the ball out trying to get extra yards. The safety finished me off with a nice hit as I was going down. I jumped up instantly looking at number eight and the safety. He had a lot of mouth just like any other corner. The defense was pissed so they moved their linebackers to my side of the field. BJ threw a quick slant into the end zone to PJ.

The score is 17-0 with 9:32 left in the first quarter. Our free safety caught a diving interception and got our offense back on the field quick. The first play went to Chris. He caught the ball, made some people miss, then got game tackled. Louie signaled a screen pass, BJ dropped back in shot gun rolling out to his right making the defense pursuit to that side, then he stopped and darted a bullet to the left side of the field to me. I had three linemen blocking ahead of me. This side of the field became clear. I ran down field full speed and saw a South Wood free safety trying his best to catch up to me. His attempt was to cut me off to make an easy tackle but he failed. It became him and me, one-on -one. I dived into the end zone for an 82- yard run touchdown. The safety bumped me, hoping that I was going to retaliate for his wrong doing. I kept my cool and threw the ball to the referee. These bums can't get to me.

I blew another kiss to Grandma. I looked over and pointed at Dee Dee as I went for the sideline. Louie and I did a manly body bump in the air once we met up.

The score became 24-0 and we continued to score nonstop. We put the ball in the air and ran down their throats repeatedly with no remorse. We were aggressive and fast, quick on our feet and fast with our hands. We looked for pain, blood, and their weakness. We made sure South Wood will remember this game. Coach took me out of the game fourth quarter with 5:16 left on the clock. The game ended 67-6, too easy. We shook hands with South Wood.

There were rumors going around that some of their players wanted to fight with us, so our school security guards and police stood around close enough to stop any altercations. I laughed and talked to some of the guys that I knew. It was a pleasure beating them but it was more business though. I just wanted a little more competition, that's all. I walked around the field talking to the players and coaches.

A sports reporter stops me in my tracks and asked me if he could ask me some questions about the game for the sports section in the newspaper.

"You have 376 receiving yards, 18 catches, and four touchdowns. What's the feeling like?" The reporter asked.

"I feel great, it's always a great feeling after you get a victory. The stats are nice but my main focus was to come out tonight and execute on every play with my team, and that's exactly what we did," I replied.

"How big of a role did your quarterback play in your stats in tonight's game?"

"BJ played a major role, everything moves through him. He made it easy for me to score up and down that field all game long. He's an elite high school football player and he's on the rise for greatness."

"Who do you think were the key players tonight?"

"Everyone was a key player tonight, even the coaches, the fans, and the guys who were standing on the sidelines cheering us on. We are all one big family!" I replied back.

"Thank you for your time Mr. Rodgers," said the reporter.

"Thank you," I said as I jogged off the field.

I put my helmet back on and smacked hands with the people who waited and cheered for me as I walked through to get to the locker room. My team was goofing around in the locker room once I got down there.

Coach Louie walked in a few minutes after I did and gave us a short speech.

"That's one team down and many more to go, enjoy this win tonight with your family, be safe, and be here bright and early in the a.m. ready to focus on Reese High."

The locker room became louder after Coach

was done talking. Coach put both of his hands on my shoulders with a tight grip then walked away. I got dressed and went to the front of the school where Dee Dee was waiting on me. She jumped in my arms the moment she saw me and told me how she kept cheering for me throughout the whole game as we walked home. Then we noticed a black navigator pulled up on the side of us.

"I think you did enough running and walking for today, hop in guys," Coach Louie said.

I was actually happy to see him because I didn't really feel like walking. Dee Dee and I got in and made it home after he bought us dinner. I felt relieved, all I wanted was a full stomach and to rest my tired legs. Food was on my mind ever since the game ended. I took a shower and had my feet resting on three pillows while watching *Sports Center* until I fell asleep.

I caught a charley horse in the middle of the night that disturbed me out of my sleep but I had to stay calm and relax so it could go away. The next morning I woke up to a very bad smell, spoiled milk and cheese, the electricity was off. There wasn't much to eat in the refrigerator but the things that were left in there smelled pretty bad. My first guess was Mom forgot to pay the bill or just hasn't gotten paid yet. I couldn't stand the smell so I sent Dee Dee to her friend's house as I was off to practice.

I arrived at practice around 8:15. Coach had the Chicago sports section of the *Sun-Times* news article hanging up in his office. It had my picture on the cover jumping over one of South Wood's defenders, I started to smirk once I saw it. I looked pretty good but I wanted to act like it wasn't a big deal to me. Coach was happier than I was of course, you would've thought they put him on the cover the way he's acting. He went on and on about how much I've grown since my freshman year.

"I knew you were born to be a star," Louie said.

I giggled then went on to get dressed. Practice was competitive all over again and my teammates called me Superstar the whole practice. We have Reese High next on our schedule, their record was 2-7 last season. Everyone knows they have no chance against us but we approach every team the exact same way.

Practice made me tired and drowsy and I have math homework that I don't see myself doing. Louie had us running the bleachers and doing suicides on every line the whole field. After practice I walked home with BJ and a few other players. By time I made it in the house, it was around 12:00 in the afternoon.

I picked Dee Dee up from her friend's house and walked to the store. We took a walk around the park afterwards, talking about the dreams we have. Dee Dee is anxious for basketball season, she wants to be the next big thing in basketball. I think the way I play inspires her to be a better athlete at her own game. I have so much faith in my little sister, I want her to be the best in anything and everything she does. I can see us both on *ESPN* being talked about daily. They're going to call us the super siblings.

I hate Mondays. I wasn't in the mood for class either, but I was looking forward to having practice. A few of my teachers talked about my performance at the game Friday and even the security guards around the school called me Clutch the Man. I remained humble all week, nothing gets to my head. My Algebra 2 teacher cared less about all the excitement, in my eyes she's evil. I feel like every math teacher is evil and out to hunt me.

I had a hard time avoiding the girls that kept talking about the game, I call them groupies. Around lunch time I caught a slight headache and I wasn't in a very good mood so I kept quiet. I got up to throw away my food tray after eating a little.

Something told me to look across the lunchroom, I think it was my conscience. I looked up and saw that mixed girl that I ran into before practice last week. I instantly walked over to where she was and suddenly my headache became slighter.

"So we meet again huh?" I said as I gave her a gentle tap on the shoulder.

"Yes I guess so although you're the one who didn't know my name," she replied back as she turned my direction.

I felt nervous, mixed with a lot of other feelings that I've never felt before. We had a normal conversation. She was sitting with a lot of unknown people, I didn't care about that though, I just want to get to know the girl. I basically questioned her the whole time we talked. Her name is Nicole and she already knew my name somehow. I hope to see her again soon, I just feel like she stands out from all the other girls in West Wood. Suddenly the bell rang,

"See you around Rajon," she said as she grabbed her two notebooks and pens.

I just stood there for a moment. I felt stuck, I want that girl for some reason, but I barely even know her. I have to get her. I snapped out of the little love dream I was having and headed to class. I walked through the halls wondering if we would run into each other. I had to get my mind focused before coach Louie finds out about her.

During the school week, we watched a lot of film and put in a lot of work. I was ready for Reese High. It was another home game so you know I'm about to go ham! Black and gold jersey, number one printed in all white.

"TOUCHDOWN!!! Rajon 'Clutch' Rodgers!" was all you heard within the minute in the start of the game.

We beat Reese High 77-14. I think I scored at least five times. I was actually Clutch on the field week by week. Libby High was right after Reese High and we beat them 73-0. That school is beyond bad. They talked too much smack to us to the point they weren't even focused on the game anymore, they just wanted to fight like any other undisciplined team. We all had to hold our composure and remain self-controlled. The corner that had to guard me from Libby was so determined to stop me, they gave me some slight competition but nothing too serious.

We are 3-0 and we have Sherman High in week four who's also 3-0. This game will be something good to really focus on. It's also the fourth week of school so the work is becoming more of a challenge. I think I failed my English test but I'll just hope for the best and prepare for the worst.

Nicole and I have been sitting together in lunch daily. We've really gotten to know each other well and I can tell we have a thing for each other. The other girls get jealous when they see Nicole and me walking and talking together in lunch. I give her more attention than any other girl in the school, even my teachers. It's a must that I keep an extra eye for Coach Louie. If Nicole and I are walking and I spot him down the hall, I instantly drop my books and tell her that I'll catch up with her later or next period, just so Louie won't see us together. He might think she will knock my focus for the field, which is completely false.

The days my homework gets out of hand I meet Nicole in our school library after practice. We spend more time smiling at each other than on our lesson. She always makes sure I get my work completed though. That's something I need since I hate school and homework so much.

Thursday was our pregame walk-through before playing Sherman High. Coach gave us our game jerseys after practice. I wanted Nicole to wear one of my jerseys to school tomorrow. I knew I was meeting her at the library, so I tried my best to get dressed swiftly. Before speeding out the door but Coach Louie called me.

"Clutch!!!" I was praying Louie didn't want anything important.

He just wanted to inform me on what schools were interested in me. He gave me a huge yellow envelop filled with letters. I tried my best to rush the conversation. All I could think about was Nicole waiting on me. I had a feeling he knew I was in a hurry to get somewhere. I got another feeling that Coach was treating me like I'm his own son or something.

"Is everything alright?" Louie asked.

"Yes Coach, everything is great."

When I made it to the library Nicole was sitting there reading. I tried to wipe the little sweat I had resting on my forehead with my shirt before she saw me. I tried to walk smoothly so I could sneak behind her and put my hands over her eyes.

"Guess who," I whispered in her right ear.

"The person that I've been waiting on for three long years," she replied.

I laughed and sat down.

"I have a surprise for you," I said while reaching in my practice bag. I pulled out my jersey and held it up. She had a pretty smile on her face. She made me blush.

"Do I get to wear it tomorrow for the game?" She asked as she took it out my hand.

I shook my head up and down. We joked around and got some homework done. I really felt the connection between Nicole and me. She's a girl I can really be myself around and just laugh. I see her in my future on draft day, maybe.

I didn't realize how late it got. We gathered all of our things and left, I ended up walking her all the way home. She lives right by the school, at least four blocks over. It was 8:23 when we made it to her house. She had the best house on the whole block, although it's a regular neighborhood like any other block in the city of Chicago, busy and trashy with bums pushing shopping carts, cats running around everywhere, loose pit bulls running wild and crazier things to see. I'm starting to think her parents have very good jobs just from the appearance of her house. I didn't really want to act like her house was a big deal because she might think I live in someone's basement or something. I didn't expect anything more from her than a hug. She gave me kiss on the cheek that made me feel warm on the inside.

I asked myself if we were rushing things on my

way home, I don't think we are. I actually really like this girl. I know I told myself I don't want or need a girlfriend at the moment, but she's different and we are just friends for now anyway. Girls are hard to trust these days, they say they love you one day, then the next day they just want to be friends for good. The loyal ones are hard to find, it's either that, or they are in places hiding where guys like myself don't really look. I just want a confident young woman that is willing to respect herself and me at the same time, honestly I just want someone who's cultured and educated.

    I was right down the street from my apartment complex when I spotted Mark. I couldn't believe my eyes. There he was, hanging in the street dressed differently like he was raised by a set of some crack head parents. I stared at him as I walked passed. The streets were busy with cars flying passed with bright flashing lights.

Third Quarter

  I suddenly decided to stop for a moment, I hesitated then called his name.

"Yooo Mark," I yelled across the street in a destructive tone.

  He looked over looking to see who I was then he jogged towards my direction, he had a surprised look on his face. He looked rough with a disturbing smell to follow.

"My main man Clutch, how you feeling Superstar?" He asked as he looked excited to see me.

  He tried to go on and on how he heard about me doing well in my last few games. I cut him off before he could even say anything else.

"Look, get off these streets man, this shit ain't you and you know it. I know the real you, them punks over there don't know the real you like I do."

The smile on his face faded away.

"Man I'm iight where I'm at, school ain't for everybody. I ain't like you dude. I don't have the heart to be like you Clutch," he said.

"You gon' get yourself killed Mark."

 He flashed his shirt up a little to show me a gun. I

frowned at him.

"What you doing with that, stupid?" I asked.

"Protection," he said.

"What happen to the slot receiver I used to know, the person that used to always say he's better than me, what happen to him?" I asked.

Jerry and the rest of his guys walked up.

"Sorry to interrupt you guys' little family reunion but umm Mark we gotta go make this move real quick," Jerry said.

"Iight den we gone then," Mark said as he walked off and looked back at me.

This guy has completely changed. I'm just pissed off at his actions, he's going down a dark path and needs to get a hold on his life quick. Deep down inside he's a very good kid. His grandma will break her neck to see him finish high school and attend a good college. I'm just not getting why he picked his last year in high school to drop out and act like a dummy on these streets. His senior year! He had one more year left. I need to see what's going on in his head before it's way too late. Last thing God can take from me is someone I care about and Mark is on that list so he needs to wake up soon. I have always been a positive role model to him. He's like the brother I never had. Mom will accept Mark before any of my other friends.

I walked the whole way home thinking about Mark and how stupid he was. I arrived quickly and the lights were back on. I guess Mom paid the bill. Dee Dee was asleep by time I got in. I woke her up after I got out of the shower and ate a small meal. I gave her my other away jersey for the game. I told her about Nicole. She thought it was cute that I took the time out to have a little focus on a girl instead of football all the time. She asked lots of questions so I told her everything I knew about Nicole and she became even more anxious to meet her the more I talked. I can't wait to see if my little sister and Nicole will sit together at the game tomorrow.

After our conversation I laid down and called Nicole on the house phone. We talked on the phone until about 12.00 in the morning, I nearly blushed the whole time talking to her. We have a few things in common. Eventually she suggested that I get some rest so I can play well tomorrow night and I did just that.

The next morning I woke up thanking God for how far He has brought me through life. After getting ready for school, I was ready to walk out the door. I plugged my headphones into my mp3 player and walked out the door. I'm game day focused and greeting everyone on the way to school was like a routine. Everyone in the neighborhood knew it was game day like always. Most will be there and the rest will hear about it. I walk these streets on game day feeling like the man, on a serious note, I am the man. This city is mine! Who's going to stop me!?

I saw Nicole in the hall after fourth period wearing my jersey. I could've passed out when I saw her, that girl had it going on!

"That's a nice jersey, where you get it from?" I asked her in a sarcastic way.

"I think I found it lying on the ground behind the school," she replied back.

We both laughed as I gave her a hug. I wanted to go in for the kill and kiss her, but then I think I'll be moving way too fast if I did that. We had lunch eighth period and lots of people asked me if we were dating throughout the whole day, even teachers. I told all of them the same thing, that she's just a good friend.

I was hoping Coach Louie didn't see her but I know he did. When he saw me, he gave me a weird look and told me to stay focused. Whatever he meant by that, I'm focused. I thought about the game in all of my classes.

I was in Algebra 2 about to die from boredom! I just don't understand anything we do in that stupid class. I feel so stupid when I'm given a test to do on my own. I might understand one or two questions out of 20- something questions. Sometimes I don't even copy the notes on the board my teacher puts up because I don't get that either. I'm not a smart person, I just have a whole lot of sense. I think I can get far enough in life with that, maybe, maybe not.

Sherman High was on my mind for the rest of

the day. Game time approached immediately after the last bell rang. Sherman is just another school not knowing what they are getting themselves into, although they're undefeated but who cares. They're going to get this work by any means!

Five minutes before kickoff, with the stands filled with students and staff, I spotted Dee Dee and Nicole sitting together just as I planned. I told Nicole where Dee Dee usually sits so everything worked out perfectly. I tuned everything out and had a quick talk with God and my grandma on one knee:

> "Thank you God for giving me the strength to make it here this day and be able to compete with such a great team and coaches, I thank you so much, thank you God. Please watch over me as I attempt to rise up and release all this hard work that rests inside of me. I love you Grandma, everything I do is for you, and I truly hope you are smiling down at me. Watch me work, save me a spot in heaven. Love you, amen."

My game face is on. After the first quarter, Sherman High stayed on us and that's what we wanted. The score was tied 21-21 and my jersey is dirty already. Their defense is real good. I had seven catches and one touchdown so far. Halftime score became 28-28, I scored one last time on a quick slant with three seconds left on the clock right before half. Coach Louie was hyped in the locker room. He told us the few mistakes we had and what we could improve on in the second half. Nothing too bad though.

"These guys want war so let's give it to them. Their linebackers wanna blitz so we must get the ball into our receiver's hands on screen plays and over the top until they choose to decide to stay home," Coach Louie yelled with enthusiasm.

    We went over more plays and talked about their offense. Third quarter was just another battle, it was third and long on their 40- yard line and we needed a first down bad. Coach called for a screen play on both sides of the field, which means BJ had a choice to either hit PJ or me. My corner played seven yards off, that was enough for me to create space by making a few moves and get up field for the first. The corner that had to guard me looked confident, he was calling out plays like he was a big shot or something, he must be a captain of the defense, he had to be. The ball was snapped, I took three steps back waiting for the ball to be released in my direction. BJ pumped, faked to me, then threw it to PJ. He caught it and gained nine yards, still not enough for the first down though. It became fourth and one. Louie signaled us to stay on the field to go for it. I felt like it was a smart idea if he really wanted to win this game.

    The next play was to Daniel. He gained seven yards moving through defenders, enough for the first down. We were back in action and we have business to take care. The score is 35-28. We scored four plays later with a five- yard out route to Chris, along with an extra point but they still stayed with us, 43-28. Time is ticking fast. Their offense moved down the field like it was that easy. They got an easy score to close the gap a little on the score board. They succeeded on an extra point attempt. We ended up punting a while later, and the plays we attempted left Sherman High with no choice but to punt the ball. Chris was the return man, he called for a fair catch so we started on our own 20- yard line and I gained 30 yards on second.

The next play we shot ourselves in the foot, I guess it was some kind of confusion between Daniel and BJ with the handoff because for some reason the ball ended up on the ground leaving Sherman High to recover it for a touchdown. They decided to kick a field goal instead of an extra point. The game got serious in the fourth with 3:23 left on the clock. The score became 43-43, but before going onto the field, I looked back and saw Nicole looking directly at me with a hopeful look on her face.

Coach Louie grabbed my helmet and told me, "It's clutch time."

That got me hyped up real fast. I looked at the clock, strapped up my helmet then blew a kiss to God while running onto the field. The corner on my side was creeping up for a jam at the line. I've been doing short routes all game so he must not know what I can do down field. The ball was snapped, BJ threw it to me on a six- yard hitch route. The corner wrapped me up and the outside linebacker finished me off. It was a pretty good hit because I didn't plan on being brought down easy. We were moving at a fast pace.

The clock went down to 2:10 as we moved down the field. Louie kept running the same play over and over again. That was a very smart move because of the way we kept gaining more and more yards from giving the rock to Daniel. They decided to cheat their safety up a little.

The clock went down to 1:28 now. I think this is the play I've been waiting for all night. Coach signaled a punch to his chest. That meant all the receivers go deep. BJ gave me the nod I was looking for, that meant take it to the house. My corner was smart, he knew to back up and watch the deep pass. He was pretty fast so I knew I wouldn't really out run him too much. The ball was snapped, time was running out. I got off the line quick, BJ dropped back and got hit instantly by their middle linebacker. Louie called timeout before any more time faded away. Our offensive line coach was pissed, he yelled at our linemen telling them to block. BJ wasn't hurt too badly, he's a pretty tough kid. Coach called the same play, but he recommended pass protection to give BJ enough time to release the ball. As we jogged back onto the field, I told BJ to pump fake then release. He acted like he didn't understand what I was saying and I didn't explain either, I just wanted him to do as I said.

I got set and waited for the ball to be snapped. My corner was seven yards off, that's perfect. The ball was snapped and I ran down the field for another hitch route. My corner bit hard on it and came up to make a play. BJ pumped fake as I told him to do as I took off down field for a fade leaving him in my dust. BJ released the ball in the air.

It's so beautiful the way it's just spinning through the wind. I ran fast as I could down the field. My heart is pounding, I'm breathing fiercely with sweat in my eyes. I could barely see the ball because of all the sweat running down my forehead. My eyes got even bigger as I reached my right hand out far enough to catch the ball. I stumbled and almost lost my balance but I kept my footing and ran all the way to the end zone.

"TOUCHDOWN!!!! Mr. Clutch Rodgers, 82-yard catch for a West Wood Lions score!" The announcer exclaimed.

The crowd almost blew out my ear drums. My team rushed into the end zone to congratulate me. I felt like a king. That's game baby. The final score became 43-37. Sherman High fans were upset, of course, I could tell. A sports reporter approached me with cameras behind him. I shook hands with the Sherman High players and talked to their coaches.

"Rajon can I borrow a little of your time?" the reporter asked.

I walked over to him.

"It was a very close game reflecting on the score board, how difficult was the win over Sherman High tonight?"

"It wasn't easy at all, I can tell you that but when you believe in yourself along with God, then anything is possible. We knew we had competition on this field tonight from the start of the game. I have a tremendous amount of respect for Sherman High. They came out on our field ready to compete with us but we were expecting the game to turn out the way it did. With a W, but not an easy one," I said.

"You've finished the game tonight with 20 catches and 219 yards on the ground. Please describe how difficult it was to perform the way you did tonight with Sherman's strong built defense."

"I don't look at my stats as a difficulty at all. I honestly don't focus on my stats during the game, I just play ball and make big plays to the best of my ability. When I put on my cleats and strap up my helmet, my purpose is to leave a mark and make sure that my defenders will remember my footsteps when I leave this field. My main focus was getting a win for this team and my community and that's what we all did together," I said.

"I notice you stated 'we,' but you're the one that ended the game with a game- winning catch, how does that feel?"

"This team ended the game with a game- winning play. It wasn't just all me. I give all glory to God and this great team. This quarterback that I have is something special, he's unbelievable, my coaches are wonderful, the support I have on the field gives me the energy and the boost to wanna keep striving for greatness, this win was a team effort and we just wanna remain focused and humble for our next competition battle."

"Thanks a lot Rajon," the reporter said.

"Thank you," I said as I jogged off the field.

      BJ got interviewed also. I was searching for Dee Dee and Nicole as I jogged through the crowd. I took a few pictures with some people and signed a few shirts and footballs. I enjoy all the attention I receive after games. Dee Dee raced to me and hugged me and Nicole was right behind her. This was the best feeling ever. The only person that was missing was Mom and my father if he's even still alive.

"Good game Clutch, or should I say Beast," Nicole said.

"Well thanks," I replied.

Mark walked up out of nowhere.

"My main man Clutch, how you feeling Superstar?" Mark asked.

He sounds like a broken record, repeating the same stuff every time he sees me.

"I know she ain't with you. Well aren't you gonna introduce me to this beautiful lil thang here?" he sneered to me as he viewed her whole body with his sneaky little eyes.

I didn't really want him meeting her. He smelled like

93

weed, that's what pissed me off the most.

"Mark this is Nicole." Mark reached for her hand. "Nicole, this used to be someone I thought I knew," I said in a stubborn way.

She tried reaching to shake his hand but I softly grabbed her hand refusing to let him touch her. His facial expression changed.

Jerry called Mark, "Time is money."

"So it's like that huh," Mark said.

"Yeah, I guess so, be safe out there man," I said as I walked off.

To me personally, I find it strange how someone can play a certain role one day then they wake up one another and be someone completely different.

In the locker room all the guys talked about my one-hand catch. Coach Louie hugged me which made the moment awkward because it felt like a father and son moment. These are the times I think about my dad and where he could be. He told me to wait around so he could drop me off at home. I knew I had Nicole and Dee Dee waiting on me. I really wish I had my own wheels so that would really make things much easier although I enjoy walking for good leg exercise. I stepped out to let them know Coach Louie was taking all of us home. They were laughing and joking around.

"What's the joke, I wanna laugh too," I said as I came

out the school gym doors.

"We were just laughing about how you look in your tight uniform pants that's all," Nicole said as she giggled.

That's so cliché for girls to talk about something like that.

"Your one- hand catch was even better," Nicole said.

I smiled. Nicole was fine with Louie driving her home. I was just nervous about Louie meeting Nicole for the first time that's all. Who knows how he's going to feel about us.

Nicole and Dee Dee waited in the gym as I went back down to the locker room to wait on Louie. It was getting kind of late. I caught him in his office as he talked to the other coaches. I didn't want to tell him about Nicole around them.

"Superstar," Coach White said as I walked in.

The other coaches laughed and clapped a little. Louie asked them to excuse us, he treats me like a god or something. I told him about Nicole without holding back, no hesitation at all. His facial expression became clueless. I told him how much she keeps me focused and how she will never interfere with my game on the field. From the look on his face and the things he was saying, I felt like he understood me and everything I expressed. I also told him how she's waiting for us along with Dee Dee.

"We don't wanna keep them waiting, let's go," Louie said.

I nervously introduced the two of them. He questioned her so he could get to know her better as he drove then we all talked about the game after a while. Louie stopped by Subway and got everyone a sandwich. He chooses to get me Subway before any other food to keep me fit and healthy during the season. He says I don't need fried food around this time of the year. He took Nicole home then next was Dee Dee and myself. Dee Dee told Louie thanks for everything before she got out his truck. Coach asked me if my lights came back on yet. My only question was how he knew our lights were off in the first place. That was a pretty weird moment but I was too tired to even care about it. He changed the subject quickly talking about my performance on the field tonight.

After a warm shower, I just had to call Nicole to see how she felt about Louie. My coach gets kind of scary sometimes. She told me Louie acts like a dad more than a coach. I agreed, but it's all love and he just wants the best for me. We talked about our homecoming dance that's coming up shortly the whole night. I even got to really know more things about her. Her dad is a big time drug dealer in our part of Chicago. I'm pretty sure I know him or have seen him around before. A lot of drug dealers around Chicago knows about me and how good I am with the ball in my hands. That probably explains why her house is so nice. I set my alarm for practice before we fell asleep on the phone.

      Practice felt like it was getting harder. We are now 4-0, our fourth game was homecoming. I've never seen so much West Wood pride in my life. Alumni surrounded the field and watched us do damage. After the victory it was party time. The homecoming dance was a night to remember. Coach Louie took me to a casual clothing store to get me fitted for the dance that night. I was dressed like I was attending the NFL draft. An hour before the dance started, Louie took me by a barbershop around the corner from my home to get me lined up. The barbers in the shop knew who I was the moment I walked through the door. I felt like I was in an interview the whole time I was in there. After rushing home, I took a shower and was ready to go. It felt good being in dress clothes, all I could think about was my name being called on draft day.

      After I got dressed, Coach Louie showed me how to tie a tie. That same awkward feeling came back around again.

"I really appreciate you Coach."

"I'll always have your back Clutch," Louie replied.

He gave me some kind of fancy cologne that I couldn't pronounce but it smelled good though. On my way to the dance, we stopped by to pick up Nicole.

"Here take this with you," Louie handed me a black rose.

I stepped out of the truck and went to go ring her doorbell. I took a deep breathe wiping the sweat from my hands onto my pants leg. A lady opened the door.

"Hi I'm Rajon. I'm here to escort Nicole to our homecoming dance," I said as I reach my hand out.

"Well hello young man, you are the one I hear so much about, come on in and have a seat, Nicole will be right down," the lady said politely.

"Now please take good care of my daughter and make sure she makes it back home safe and sound before midnight," the lady said.

"Yes Ma'am I'm very grateful and pleased to be taking your daughter to our school dance, I will make sure she gets back home before midnight," I said as I sat there eager to see Nicole.

"Nicole you better hurry up before I steal him," she yelled upstairs.

I did a fake laugh. The moment Nicole came downstairs I became kind of nervous. She's the most beautiful young lady I've ever laid eyes on.

"For you," I said as I gave her the thick, dark rose.

"He's such a gentleman," the lady said.

"Okay Mom we have to go now," Nicole said.

"Well wait I want pictures," her mom replied.

Her mom took at least 50 pictures of us, in the living room and outside. Coach Louie stood outside in front of his truck like he's my driver which made me look good.

"You two look so nice together, have fun and be safe," her mom yelled.

Louie opened the door for us. We waved to her mom out of the window as we pulled off. I asked about her dad but she said he's busy. That's probably the reason why I was so nervous, I was expecting to meet him. We pulled up 45 minutes after the dance started. All students that were attending the dance needed their school I.D. to get in. By the time we got to the door I noticed that I left mine at home. The security guard welcomed me in like it wasn't a problem that I didn't have an I.D. The dance was amazing it had loud music, flashing lights, plenty of beverages and all sorts of things to eat. Nicole and I walked in holding hands. I just knew all eyes were on us. That was a night to remember.

Back to the gridiron, it feels good to be undefeated after four competitive weeks. We were the best school around. We have to win two more games in order to make it to the playoffs. I don't think that will be a problem the way Louie is working us. Away games are coming up soon. Home field advantage is everything, once a team has that then they think they have a better chance of winning. State is the goal. This is my last year playing high school football so I've been making every game count like it's my last. Week after week we took Ws and more Ws.

We proudly tortured and punished Kennedy High 83-17. I scored at least six touchdowns that game, easy! Gage Park was a joke with their green and blue jerseys, we gave them a run for their money leaving the score board 66-0. I had the biggest mouth that game. Caroline Central was a country team from the east side and we managed to bring home a W with a 42-30 score. Downey High gave us the most trouble. They came out hitting hard and running the ball fast every single play. We played just after it got done raining so there was a lot of slipping and sliding taking place but we managed to take the win for that one as well, the score ended 58-50.

My game stats have been taking over Chicago high school sports weekly. I've been on the face of different sports articles and have been talking to a lot of college coaches lately. I'm the face of high school football, baby. No one can name another high school athlete that's better or works harder than I can. I'm a dog, I'm a beast, I'm a gorilla, and I'm a savage as well. I am football.

My relationship with Nicole has gotten better as the weeks pass by. We are now eight meaning we're number one in conference and the best in the state. You put us in front of a team and we will execute until we see blood. There's nothing else to talk about. Our last regular season game was very emotional and I actually had the thought running through my head that I'll never play another regular season high school football game ever again. So my last home game, I absolutely played my heart out. We played an undefeated school called Kroc High. They are ranked number two right behind us on the map.

The second half of the game was intense. Their defense was aggressive, just the way I like it. They have the best middle linebacker in the nation and he's already committed to the University of Alabama. They call him the vicious attack dog. His hits might give you a serious headache if you meet him head on which means he plays to kill. He's mean, he's fast, and quick with his decision making. His vision is great and it's just not easy getting passed a guy like him, I like his game though. I made him miss a few times but other than that, he put some pretty nice hits on me. Their quarterback was also a big playmaker. He's a pocket passer with protective, strong linemen giving him enough time to put the ball in his receiver's hands. Their football team looked like all they eat is chicken breast and protein shakes. The last game ended 77-70.

Coach White had me on defense making plays in the whole fourth quarter. We made it through the whole regular season undefeated. After that game, we laughed and cried tears of joy in the middle of our field. Our school was proud, the coaches and staff were proud, the whole neighborhood was even more proud of us. We made it to the playoffs. I want a ring, that's the complete way to be married to the game of football at this level: a high school state ring. There were three playoff games before the state championship game.

We will know who we have to face for the first round by Monday at practice. Although we were geeked, we want to remain focused and be aware of any good team that's on our list. The playoffs are no joke. Chicago weather gets extremely cold in the month of November so you have to seriously want it bad in order to play ball between the months of November and December.

Monday my Algebra 2 teacher gave me back a graded test that I took the past week, I received a 48%. I wasn't really shocked to see a failing grade. I actually took the time to study after practice and I still received the grade that sat in front of me.

"Stay after class Rajon," Ms.Hale said to me.

Everyone sprinted out of class once the bell rang except me, of course. I sat there looking at my test with a dumb look on my face.

"Did you take the time out to study or were you too busy scoring touchdowns?" Ms.Hale asked.

"Honestly, there's really no explanation. I just don't like math, it's pointless. Most of this work is straight bull shit," I said to her.

"You don't have to like math, it's a requirement in order for you to graduate and be successful in life down the road," she said as she looked at me. "I informed your coach Rajon."

I was too busy staring at that gigantic ugly mole on her top lip so I wasn't really paying attention to what she was saying. She looks like a hamster or small rodent of sorts.

"You are Rajon Rodgers in my classroom, Clutch doesn't exist in here. Your coach's main focus is you playing football, all the touchdowns you make do not excite me, your effort in this classroom does. Either you pass your next test or you will not be playing until you do pass."

      Everything she told me played over and over in my head for the rest of the day until the start of practice. I couldn't believe that lady, she's evil and she's really trying to break me. I just don't understand why though. It had to be for a reason, but I never disrespected her in any kind of way at all until today with my poor choice of words, but there's just so much a person can take until they explode. I never talk back to adults period. Mom taught me to stay in a child's place and play my role as a young man no matter what. Overall I respect my elders. To be honest, I don't even like school, I'm just here to keep moving forward in life. I know if I drop out I won't be able to play ball at the next level.

      Coach called me into his office right before practice. I knew it was about Ms.Hale and that F in her class. He sounded more concerned than she was. Louie never really gets mad at me for some odd reason. He told me to study during lunch, at night, in the morning, and any other free time I receive. Before leaving his

103

office he stopped me again.

"One more thing, is that girl getting in the way of your focus? Because if she is then you might wanna-"

I instantly had to cut him off. "No Coach, she keeps me focused. This grade doesn't really make sense to me." I couldn't believe he even took it there.

"Well ok, just checking."

The words Ms.Hale said to me played in my head over and over again all through practice. Although it didn't knock me off my game. I had a few drop balls but nothing too major. Every great receiver drops passes sometimes, although it won't be that often. During the week I studied my butt off, late nights, early mornings, and all through the day. It's just not clicking into my brain the way I need it to. I don't like math, how many times do I have to tell these people that? But I know I have to suck it up for playoffs. This test will either make me or break me, I have to compete with it either way. The competitive edge I have on the field needs to translate into the classroom. It's a must that I play in the first playoff game. There's a very thin line between want and will, and I will pass this test. At the end of practice Coach informed us on who we were facing in the first round of the playoffs: Drucil High School.

That school is kind of tough, we lost to them last season in the second round of the playoffs. It was a close game but they pulled through with the W and sent us home with sad faces and broken hearts. We watched film on them for a while after practice. Coach kept the quarterbacks, receivers, and defensive backs for an extra practice after the film session. It was something like a seven- on- seven to focus on the small stuff that could help us win our next game. We followed Coach to the game field under the lights. Coach is serious about beating Drucil.

"No dropped passes, no missed tackles, no lazy route running, we must score every chance we get. The seven- on- seven ran for about an hour and 15 minutes. I caught passes from BJ and our backup quarterback, Dennis. He's good, but he cracks under pressure whenever we need him the most. That's the main reason why he doesn't see the field on game day. BJ can handle it all, that's why he's our starter.

After practice I got home and looked over my notes. It's kind of hard to study something that you don't even understand, I'll still try my best though. Nicole tried her best to do whatever she could to help me out. I didn't really want her to find out that I'm not that smart. We talked on the phone for about 35 minutes but she wanted me to study instead of being on the phone with her all night. I threw my notebook on the floor and turned on *Sports Center*.

A knock sounded at our front door. I got up to answer it with a confused look on my face. I pray to God it's Mom. My hopeful face expression changed once I saw who it was. It's just Mark. He stormed in sweating nervously.

"Bro I need your help man."

"Calm down what's wrong?"

"Can I please stay here for a few hours?" Mark asked looking like he just had just seen a ghost.

"Man what did you do," I replied.

"Nothing man, I ain't do it man, it was nothing," he stuttered.

  I knew he was in some huge mess just by his ugly facial expression. Last thing I want is him bringing drama around me, he stinks too. I told him to have a seat and relax. We both sat in the living room watching television. I tried to study but it didn't work out too well. I kept a close eye on him, he peered out the window every five minutes, slightly sweating in a dingy black jacket. He tried getting comfortable but he was too busy fidgeting the whole time. I just knew this guy was in some deep trouble, I could feel it.

"Do you want me to walk you home Bro?" I asked him as I got up off the couch.

"No!" He yelled in a terrifying way. "I mean, no because you have to rest, we want you to be safe and get good rest so nothing bad ever happen to you."

At this moment, I'm scared for his life. Something or someone is really after him. He went for the door.

"Where you going man?" I asked him.

"I'm about to run to the store real fast," he replied as he struggled to zip up his jacket.

"Naw man, if you hungry I can-." he cut me off before I could even finish.

"Naw man, thanks I'm good, I'm not even hungry Bro," he said.

"Then why are you going to the store if you're not hungry?" I asked.

"Just to see what they selling, you know?"

"No I don't know," I said to him.

I tried getting him to just stay longer than he planned to, but that didn't work too well.

"Yo Clutch," he said before walking out the door.

"Wassup man," I replied.

"I love you Bro, you know that right?"

"Yea, I love you too Bro." He took off out the door "Mark!"

He stopped and turned around to look at me.

"Be safe man," I said.

He shook his head and went on his way. I wanted to follow after him but just didn't. I got in the shower then fell back for the night. I wanted to dream about making big plays in the playoffs.

Tuesday morning I wasn't really feeling school too much. My mind was loaded with this math test I have coming up Wednesday, Mark and his problems, Drucil defense, and so much more. I wish I had Mom in my corner at this moment in my life. I'm starting to think she just doesn't love me the way I thought she did. My mood changed, next period I have Ms.Hale's class. Anger overcame me and I felt like taking a brick with me to her class, it's just that bad. When the bell rang, I wanted to walk as slow as I could and be late, but I knew it would only make things worse between us.

I walked in and sat in the back of the room. We started writing down notes from the board, just more bull crap that I don't understand or care about. I wanted to throw my textbook at her forehead and walk out of the classroom. I kept cool and I copied every number and word from the board, I even took my time to write neatly. Ms.Hale called me up to the board so I could attempt a problem that she wrote out. I got up and walked to the board slowly.

"Today Rajon," Ms. Hale yelled.

When I got up there the problem read: *Find constants A and B that make the equation true. $2x-9/x^2-x6=A/x-$*

$3+B/x+2$. I stared at the problem for a while, standing there pretending like I knew what I was doing.

"Mmmmmhh let's see here," I said as I looked at the board even longer.

"Boy could you hurry up, dang you taking all day like you slow or something," a girl named Keisha blurted out. She's a real ghetto individual with no respect for herself. I looked over at her for a moment

"Girl shut up and comb yo dirty weave before I call animal control on you," I replied. The classroom laughed.

"Boy don't make me start on you," she said.

"Take your seat Rajon and sit quiet," Ms. Hale yelled.

"Ugly ass little boy," Keisha mumbled.

"Dirty ass lil rat," I blurted back at Keisha. "You know what Keisha, I don't even know why you like to open your mouth to talk. The jump man on your Jordan's looks like he's shooting a free throw and your weave looks like a wig that was donated to you."

The class room turned into a circus once that came out of my mouth. I can tell Ms.Hale was getting mad.

"Hope you are ready for your test tomorrow Mr. Sir," Ms.Hale said.

"Yeah I'll be ready," I said as I sat down.

That test haunted me throughout the whole entire day.

It was sitting right in front of me before I even knew it. The classroom is completely empty. It was just Ms. Hale, the test, and me.

"I will grade your test as soon as you are finished, so don't rush off too fast Speedy," Ms.Hale said.

She made the test harder than it was before. It looked like college questions or something. I completed the test in about 20 minutes, I knew because I watched the clock every five minutes. I sat the test in front of Ms.Hale nervously. I wrote as neatly and clearly as I could, I even put a smiley face in the top right corner of my paper just for her. I sat down and watched her mark my paper with a red pen. She was shaking her head in shame. I felt sick to my stomach.

"You failed Rajon, you will not be playing."

I put my head down on the desk. I'm tired of this grumpy lady.

"Can I have my test back to see what I did wrong at least?" I asked her.

"Sure, here you go, but I want it back before you walk out," she replied. I really wanted to know why she wouldn't let me take it home to fix my corrections.

"Can I retake it right now?" I asked.

"No you cannot, you failed, end of story, and have a nice day."

      I gave her the test back and headed to practice. I don't care anymore, I couldn't care anymore. My brain hurts just from attempting that stupid test. Man fuck that test. I walked to the practice field without getting dressed. I thought about Ms.Hale saying I'm not playing in the next game. Everyone asked me why I wasn't dressed when I stepped foot on the field. I didn't answer. I just felt like punching a brick wall. I feel like I'm letting the team down. I told Coach about my situation with the failing grade and what Ms.Hale said to me.

"Let's go," Coach said.

      I followed him into the school. Ms.Hale was just gathering up her things when Coach and I walked into her classroom.

"I was expecting you Coach, but not this soon," Ms. Hale said.

"I bet you were," he replied back. "May I take a look at the test?" Coach asked her.

"I'm afraid not Coach," Ms.Hale said.

"And why is that?" Coach asked again.

Ms.Hale didn't really have a valid reason of why she's not able to show Coach Louie the test. She said she just packed it up and misplaced it. Now I know something is really up with this evil witch. Coach picked up a picture that rested on Ms.Hale's desk of her kids. They looked like they were about my age.

"If it's ok to ask, where do your children attend school Ms.Hale?" Coach asked.

"My daughter attends the University of Texas, and my other two are still in high school, now if you two gentlemen excuse me, I have to get home to my family," Ms.Hale said.

"And what high school do they attend Ms.Hale?" Coach asked with a concerned tone in his voice.

I became very confused about the situation.

"They both attend Drucil High School," Ms.Hale said with a guilty, dumb look on her face.

112

"We got your ass! Everything makes sense to me now!" I yelled.

This lady is out of her mind.

"Do your sons play football at, Drucil High School?" Coached asked her.

I think Ms.Hale knows she's busted.

"Rajon go get dressed for practice," Ms.Hale said.

"No Lady, my name is Clutch and you better remember that."

"Go get dressed Clutch," Coach Louie said.

I wasn't surprised at all. This lady tried to make me miss the game against her sons so they could have a better chance of winning the state playoffs. That's all I needed to know, it's war time now. I'm even more pissed.

Timeout

It's finally the Friday I've been waiting for. The first round of the playoffs of my senior season is finally here. It's either fight to the end and give everything you got, or it's go home and feel sorry for yourself. I'm not going home, not without a fight at least. The bleachers are filled on both sides of the stadium. It's game time baby. The color of Drucil jerseys got my attention the moment I saw their players arrive on the field, they look pretty okay in their blue and yellow patterned uniform. Despite the uniforms, I wanted to know what positions Ms. Hale's sons play. I guess I'll find out later on in the game. They have to pay for their mother's poorly attempted actions. My main focus is winning though.

This game was like any other competitive game we had this season. We scored, they scored, it was an evenly matched game back to back scoring all the way until nine minutes left in the fourth quarter. I'm hot so I need the ball every rip. Our defense is out on the field while Louie has the playbook in my hands going over the plays with us. As Coach tries his best to talk over all the noise, we suddenly hear:

"Touchdown number nine, Josh Hale!"

I looked up from the sideline and spotted his jersey. There he is, Ms. Hale's son. He plays the same position as I do. I glanced at him all game but never paid close attention to the name on the back of his jersey. Now all I have to do is find his brother. Drucil tied the game 42-all. After running the ball, we stroked right back with a 52-yard pass to Chris. We tried going for a two- point conversion, but didn't pull through, but it's okay. The score became 48-42 and we have plenty of time to keep the lead with only 5:32 left in the game. Our defense took the field with confidence.

"Clutch!" Louie yelled. "Listen Son, I'm not teaching you to retaliate although retaliation is related to nature. Revenge is not a key to open doors in life, but this is business. Go play safety."

He called timeout and put me in. I'm pretty familiar with playing free safety. I threw on my helmet and took the field.

"Welcome to the wild side," Travis said.

We shook hands then got set out on the field. I knew exactly what Coach wanted me to do. I got focused as Drucil raced to the line to get set. Defense is no joke. They ran the ball the first three plays not gaining much. Drucil's running back ended up on the ground before I reached him play after play, it's third and twelve.

"Play twenty!" Coach White yelled out to me.

It was my job to tell the defense the play I had on my wrist band.

"Check lion! Check lion!" I yelled to my teammates.

That meant cover three. I kept an eye on Ms. Hale's son, he has no clue what's coming his way. I'm pretty sure Ms.Hale is somewhere in the stands watching nervously. The ball was snapped, he took off downfield. Drucil quarterback looked in his direction, but threw it to another receiver. Travis made a clean hit almost forcing a fumble. Time went down to 3:18. They got the first down on the 50-yard line. We need a turnover to be safe. If Drucil scores, then we will have a very slight chance to score. A few plays later was what I was waiting for.

The ball was released deep down field into number nine's direction. I hesitated for a moment giving him a chance to reach for the ball. Boom! I laid my shoulder pads deep into his chest. I hit that boy with everything I had in me. Who cares if he would've died? I would've just attended his funeral to show my condolences. The crowd felt his pain from the reaction they gave.

"Now you tell Ms. Hale to give me back my test because I studied hard young man," I said to number nine in a sarcastic, old grandma voice.

My team cheered me on. Louie pointed at me, I pointed back. Now there's an injury timeout, number nine laid there restless. I felt bad for him until I thought about everything his mother put me through. He was helped off the field five minutes later by his school athletic trainers. He's out for the game with a concussion. We are left in the game with 1:43 left on the clock. Drucil's starting quarterback is limping so they were forced to put in their backup. For a moment I thought I was dreaming, the back of this kid's jersey says Hale. So there you have it, Ms. Hale has a starting receiver and a backup quarterback. Time wasn't on their hands, neither ours. Drucil's backup quarterback tried throwing deep down field. The ball traveled through the air right to me. I jumped up to grab it, Travis and I both went up together not realizing we're on the same team. I managed to get a hold of it until the ball fumbled out of my possession as it hit Travis' helmet the moment I attempted to come down with it. That was the only play we needed to secure this win.

Thirty -three seconds left on the clock with one timeout left. Drucil was 27 yards away from a touchdown to win the game and send us home for the season.

The ball is snapped, Hale scrambled around looking for an open receiver. He found one.

"Touchdown Drucil!"

Their crowd went completely wild. My heart dropped as I was lost into shock. I unstrapped my helmet and fell to my knees as I watched Drucil sidelines celebrate. Drucil coaches dropped their heads. God was on their side in the game this time. There was dirty laundry lying on the field which means there's a flag on the play. All the attention went directly to the referee to see what the call was. The ref started rasping his right wrist, his fist was clenched in front of his chest.

"Holding on the offense."

That makes it third and seven. We are now back in this football game, we still have hope. The clock ticked down and we called for a timeout. Drucil had time for just one more play.

"The quarterback knows how to put the ball in the end zone, we need pressure on him!" Coach White yelled.

As we jogged back on the field, I told our left defensive end to take deep. Coach White yelled at us from the sideline.

"What are they doing?" Coach White yelled to Louie.

I could hear him.

"Just wait and let's see," Louie said.

I played back from the line of scrimmage almost lined up as a corner next to Travis.

"What are you doing man," Travis whispered.

I didn't pay any attention to anyone but that ball and that quarterback. I was sweating dramatically! I knew the game was in my hands because of the changes I just made on this field.

"Get deep!" I yelled to Travis.

118

I heard Coach White's voice again, he might lose his voice from the way he's yelling. The ball was snapped, I took off full speed around the edge looking for Hale and there he was. I was so anxious to the point I tripped over my own two feet. Hale took off to the right side of the field. He's confident, I can tell. I got up as quickly as I could. He scrambled back to the left side. That's when it all happened! I took that dude out like my life was on the line. The ball came out, our linemen recovered it, and raced to our end zone down the field. Drucil teammates were in his tracks. I stood over Hale looking to help him up. I changed my mind two seconds later. He looked lifeless.

"Tell Ms. Hale I said wassup," I said while stepping over him.

That's game baby, first round belongs to us. We are closer to where we need to be. Louie grabbed my face mask once I made it to the sideline.

"Now that's what I'm talking about Son!" He screamed in my face.

I celebrated with my team, it felt good. Reporters were scattering the field the moment the clock went out. We talked about the game the whole bus ride home. Louie didn't let us get too happy, he was informed that we play Pettis Central next. It's now time to prepare for war once again. Game day felt like it was just hours away after we just heard who we were playing.

Pettis Central came at us hard. Running the ball and blocking proficiently. No matter how good Pettis Central blocked, we pulled out a 33-14 win by the end of the fourth quarter. We are now on the road to semi-finals. If we beat our next opponent, we make it to the state finals. Crandon High School is next on our hit list. Even school was better than ever. Ms. Hale hasn't been to school since that little incident. I just feel like the happiest kid alive right now.

Westwood is determined to win state. Our teachers made shirts and hoodies to support our football team. I walk in the halls and see banners on the wall of our numbers and names. Our school even started a hallway parade just for the football players and cheerleaders. I was feeling the best side of high school at this point of my life.

Nicole is my second number one fan behind Dee Dee. She's been to every game ever since we met. I really see her in my future at my college and NFL games. I always wanted my wife to be someone I grew up with. Meeting someone in college or later in life is cool, but a long journey sounds much better in my book. It's Thursday, our last playoff game is this Saturday night. Coach Louie keeps us in the film room daily, before and after practice. He even added 12 new plays to our playbook, half of the plays were mainly for me. Light hitting, lots of ball catching, route running, seven- on- sevens, team drills, and lots and lots of conditioning. Coach ran us so much that I was confused if he was a football coach or a cross country coach. We are determined as a team to win state.

The film we watched on Crandon High School didn't impress us at all. I tried my best not to fall asleep while watching their defense play. We plan to destroy that school and get them out of our way. Louie wanted us to win by at least 40, so that's what we plan to do. I was given my regular season stats after practice. I broke eight records and set six records of my own this season. They read:

Senior Year Stats

This (regular) season stats 2,432 receiving yards

108 catches

32 TDs

Career Stats 4,720 receiving yards

411 catches

129 TDs

Coach Louie gave me more letters about the division one colleges that were interested in me. Talking about leaving for college is bittersweet, I've never left the city of Chicago a day in my life. The main thing that rides my mind is who's going to keep up with Dee Dee. I really want her to be safe while I'm away. My top five colleges are Ohio State, Kentucky, Oklahoma, Oklahoma State, and Oregon. No matter where I go, I just want to play more football and compete at the next level with elite athletes.

I'm invited to the U.S Army All American Bowl, The South Bay BMW West Coast Bowl, the Top Elite Nike Seven- On- Seven, The ESPN High School Elite game, and a few more.

After practice I hung out with Nicole at her place. This was my fifth or sixth time coming over. She told me her mom won't care if she catches me in her room, this is very rare for a girl to say. Her dad was my main focus though, I don't have time to get chased with a gun days before the biggest games of my life. We sat around her room doing homework.

"I've never had a boy in my room before, you're the first," she said to me as she put the cap on her pen.

"Does that mean I'm lucky or special?" I replied.

She sat her books down and walked into my direction. The look in her eyes made my stomach drop. This girl looks like she wanted something from me, she sat on my lap facing me. Taking my notebook out my hands and gently kissing me, I wondered if I smelled like I just got out of practice but I think I smell pretty okay though. This was a real actual kiss, my heart was beating fast. I don't know if she knows, but I'm a complete virgin. I've seen movies before, but I've never actually been in action with a real girl. She started to take off my shirt and then we both slowly undressed one another. We're even moving like virgins, slow.

This girl has the softest skin I've ever touched. Her body is attracting me the most at the moment. Feeling on her gave me the relaxing confidence I needed.

"Have you ever been with a girl?" She asked me.

      I shook my head no as she made the first move. My heart started beating faster by the second, this feels like a movie or something. I would've never thought this would come in handy so soon, Coach Louie supplied me with three condoms on the first day of school. I was smart enough to keep one in my book bag just in case an unexpected moment like this happened, in case a special moment like this happened, I must say.

      This is my moment to become a man. The line Louie always joked about played over and over in my head, *it's just the motion in the ocean.* I tried my best to play smooth and just relax. She laid on her back and looked at me, I guess this is the part where the car goes into the garage slowly. I learned how to put on a condom in health class my freshman year, that really helped me out. I opened the condom, slowly ripping it open, I rolled it on then looked at her.

"Is this your first time?" I asked her.

She shook her head yes.

"Let's move at your speed, direct me where I'm going," I said while climbing on top.

She grabbed me with her cold, soft hands then inserted me into herself gently. It was so warm in there and I went with what I knew best. The palms of her hands held a tight grip to my arms at first, then she slowly slid them to my back. I kind of knew what I was doing from here, I tried to really do my thing but also make sure the atmosphere remained intimate at that same time. I kissed her soft lips slowly. At the same time I wanted to be very patient and gentle with her, even patient with myself and take my time so I don't make a fool out of myself. She kept putting her hands over her face, I don't know if it was because she's shy or embarrassed. We stayed in the same position the whole time. As I held her tight I could hear her gasp then she locked her legs around me and breathed fiercely. I felt her body shivering.

After a while I reached a climax that made me feel weak. My body felt like it was melting and I just knew this moment turned me into a mature, young man. I kissed her lips then her forehead before climbing off of her and we both laid together side by side.

"It hurt so bad right now," she said.

I got up quickly taking the condom off and watched it flush down her toilet. I got back in bed procrastinating about saying a word. I think she's in her feelings when I saw her ball up with her hand tucked in between her thighs and stomach. I'm a little nervous to look over at her.

"I have a mother and a little sister, I would be ready to kill someone if they ever took the most valuable and precious thing from either one of them and then just walked out they're life," I said to her.

I can tell she felt better from what I just said, she was just scared that I would leave her after getting in her pants. That's what every girl's scared of, I'm not like that.

I have a major amount of respect for all women, they go through way more than I can even imagine. I'm so blessed to not have a monthly situation like they do. I salute every female on earth, that's why I would never call a girl a female dog, Mom taught me very well. When a man decides to disrespect a woman by either hitting her or calling her out her name, he disrespect his mother, his sisters, aunts, grandma, and any other woman in his family. After our deep conversation I got dressed to go. I had to get home to Dee Dee, it was 10:04 so I know she's looking for me.

After tonight, Nicole and I are much closer definitely much more than friends. I thought about her almost all the way home, so much I even did a little dance once I walked out of her house. I felt like a new man, a new, new man. I had time to think the whole way home. Turning the corner down my block I spotted red and blue lights on an ambulance truck, police, and yellow tape blocking off the streets. It was almost right in front of my building.

"Clutch come quick they shot your little sister," people screamed at me.

I ran as fast as I could to the back of the ambulance truck. My whole life flashed before my eyes, I couldn't even see with all the tears in my eyes.

"Who did this?!" I screamed as loud as I could, not even being able to catch my breath.

I feel like I'm about faint at any moment. A body rested on the ground 20 feet from the truck covered with a white sheet, this person is dead whomever it is. I paused for a moment hesitating about going over to see who it was, but I went anyway. It felt like I was moving in slow motion the closer I got to the body. Squatting down and pulling the sheet back was the hardest thing I ever had to do in my whole entire life. Wiping the tears from my eyes, I recognized the face. This was one of the many guys that always told me I'm going to be a first- round pick in the NFL. I stared at him.

Coach Louie's truck pulled up. I have no idea who called him or how he even knows I was affiliated with this situation. The ambulance rushed off with Dee Dee and the only person I'm looking for an answer from at this moment is God. Another body rested on the other side covered with the same white sheet. I walked over and pulled the sheet back a little. I became traumatized the moment I saw Mark's face, I fell back not able to catch my balance. My brother is gone. The guy I grew up with, the guy I learned about the true values of life with is gone. The only person I became a better athlete with is now gone from this earth, I'm torn apart.

I can't think, nothing is making sense to me. Dee Dee is being rushed to the hospital and my best friend is dead. Coach Louie pulled the sheet back over Mark's head and grabbed me. Resting my face on his chest, drowning his shirt with tears, I'm trying to find some type of composure. I've never felt this way before. A neighbor rushed to me before I jumped in Louie's truck.

"Yo Rajon, I saw it all with my own eyes man, Mark came by looking for you and some guys came by and shot him. Your sister was just in the wrong position at the wrong time."

Moments later we arrived at the hospital, rushing through the doors, I just wanted to hear that she's going to be okay.

"Where's Dee Dee?" I yelled, over and over again until someone answered me.

I was told to wait and sign in. My anger was getting the best of me, I didn't have time to use a pen to write on a stupid sign- in sheet.

"I just want my little sister!" I yelled.

She's all I really have at this point of my life. I was held back by Louie and another male doctor. They told me she's being worked on in a big room with doctors all around her. I yelled as loud as I could, I won't continue to live on this earth without Dee Dee. I was held down by Coach Louie, he managed to keep me calm for a few hours. I finally held my composure, walking back and forth in the waiting room. People looked at me like I was crazy but had no idea what I was going through.

About four hours later we were called to come in her room. I followed the male nurse immediately, almost walking on the back of his heels. My emotions got the best of me when I arrived in Dee Dee's room , I saw she was hooked up to a lot of cables. I stood over her hoping I would wake up soon from the nightmare I was having. I pulled up a chair to sit closer to her bed as Coach Louie stood behind me.

"What's wrong with her?" I tried to mumble without breaking down into tears.

The doctor put up an X-ray on the wall.

"She was shot here," he pointed. "The bullet did major damage when it hit the spinal area. Right now she's in a deep coma and there's no telling how long it will take for her to wake up. It could be hours, days, weeks, or even months, I'll give you guys time alone," the doctor said as he walked out.

I felt sorry for Dee Dee.

"I mean why her man, what she did to anybody?" I asked. "My life has been a roller coaster. Everything goes up for a long period of time, and then drops all the way down the opposite direction out of the blue with something like this.

"Coach my whole life is messed up, the main person I think about daily is my father and he doesn't know what I go through or what he did to me. I've been hurt by him since I was five years old. The more the days go by, the deeper I'm cut by him."

"He knows how you feel," Coach Louie said as he stood up and walked towards the room window. "He knows your pain Rajon.

"He watches you play and notices you play through the pain that he caused you and your mother. You're powerful and bold, you're fearless and uncompromising with the things that have happened to you. Rajon means king, that's what you are.

"When your mother first told me she was pregnant, I felt like the heaviest weight in the world rested on my shoulders. I was scared and I thought I was a man until you came into this world. I knew then I was still a boy. Growing up, my father always told me either face my fears like a man or get rid of them. The day you were born, I had no clue of how to even hold you in my arms, I didn't even know how to feed you the first night you came home. I just knew, I had a younger me in this world."

Tears fell from my face as he spoke. He had a look of shame on his face along with tears. He knows he's guilty.

"The day in Wal-Mart was my breaking point. It was a stupid idea because I knew you were gonna be old enough to remember what was going on but I just couldn't handle what I was going through."

"Why five years later, why did you wait until I was five? You told me to never give up on anything in life!" I yelled at him.

"You right, that's what I said, and I don't know why, I still don't know. That's why I want you to be better than I was Rajon," Louie said.

"Everything makes sense now everything you do for me, everything you ever told me makes sense now," I said with disgust and anger. "Why did it take so long to tell me this? Huh? Why did it take you 13 years to feel the need to crawl back into my life?" I asked.

"I didn't want you to run away and never forgive me," he replied.

"At this moment I don't know how to even feel."

"Just tell me if you'll ever forgive me Son," he pleaded as he walked over to me. "I'll give up everything, my coaching job, the state championship, just to start over as a real father to you Rajon, please Son."

I walked out of the room and I bumped a lady who smelled like an alley on my way out, not paying attention to where I was going. I walked all the way home knowing it wasn't safe walking where I was at this time of night, but what's the worst that can happen? My life already feels like it's slowly ending. I cried almost the whole walk home. I'm stressed, I'm way too young for this shit, I don't know what to look forward to anymore. I'm just Rajon. I'm done playing football, nothing will ever excite me again like football did. I've been someone who tried to remain focused and do the right thing my whole life. Why do all these bad things happen to someone like me? I'm innocent. I was trying to make a good life for myself and things like this happen to a guy like me.

I took my time walking home, I wasn't in a rush. It was 6:32 in the morning when I arrived home, I just sat on the couch thinking about everything Louie said to me, but it made things worse. I'm still not able to accept the fact that my best friend is gone, he's not coming back ever again and I'm torn apart from that. I have the most hope for Dee Dee, she doesn't understand how much I need her, I need her here with me.

I heard a knock at the door that disturbed me. I just sat there, restless, not being able to move an inch, too many thoughts are running through my head. I walked in the bathroom and stood in the mirror for about five minutes, I didn't even recognize myself. I don't know who I am as a person anymore.

The house phone rang, but I refused to answer it. For a moment it sounded like a voice coming from the other side of the mirror and it sounds like my grandma was calling my name. She's trying to tell me something so I reached out to touch the mirror. I wanted to feel her, but she disappeared quickly when my fingers pounded the glass. I think it's just the pain in my heart crying out for her spirit to come and save me from this earth, I don't belong here anymore. Another tear fell from my face as I heard the same knock at the front door again. My vision became blurry, I tried sitting down but I still had no control. I feel really light headed and dizzy, I can't keep my eyes open.

Fourth Quarter

"Grandma!" I yelled as I opened my eyes.

I think I had a dream about her as I woke up, I found myself lying in a warm hospital bed with big, white pillows. The first person I saw was Nicole's pretty face as she stood over me holding a tight grip to my hand, kissing it. I didn't expect her to be here, I didn't even expect myself to be here.

"How are you feeling Superman?" Nicole asked me.

She seemed very concerned about me like I was hit by a car or something. Louie stepped up.

"Can I have a word with him please?" Louie asked.

Nicole looked at me and I shook my head to let her know it was okay then she walked out of the room. I tried saying something but Louie's voice controlled the conversation. It's time for me to suck it up and go get my life back. Life just hit me and now I have to strike right back.

"Shhhh, just rest Son, there's no need to say anything. You are something special Rajon."

"Coach, what time is it?" I asked, cutting him completely off. "Don't we have a game today?"

I attempted to get up but he put his strong hand gently on my chest signaling me to lay back and rest on the fluffy pillows. Everything he said to me felt irrelevant, it went in one ear and out the other. All I could think about is the game. I want to play football!

I ended up missing the game and I was depressed. I walked to Dee Dee's room every other hour checking in on her, but she's in the same condition. I feel so bad for her, she just doesn't deserve any of this. I prayed while holding her hand asking God to protect His little angel. I'm tired of crying, it seems that's all I've been doing the last few days. I tried getting some sleep but I wanted to wait until Louie got back with the news about the game. If we don't beat Crandon High School then my life will be useless. I won't be playing anymore high school football ever again. This can't be the end, we must go to state, it's just a must.

Hours later I finally dozed off. I dreamed about scoring in the state championship until I heard Louie's voice in my sleep.

"I know you don't want any more of this hospital food," Louie said.

I opened my eyes and saw him standing at the door holding a bag of food. He brought my favorite, Harold's Chicken. I woke up eating like a pig, I ate in a rush waiting to hear about the game I could tell he was hesitating to tell me. Louie asked the doctor about my condition, and the doctor suggested that I get a little more rest before being active on the field. He said a hard hit can put me to sleep quickly. I laid there patiently waiting for Coach to tell me the news.

"I have very bad news Son," he said in a gloomy way as he walked to the window.

"There's nothing I'm not prepared to hear Coach, I've heard and been through enough."

"Well, I'm sorry to say but there might not be enough room in here," Louie said as he looked around.

"I don't wanna be here anyway," I said.

"Meet your state- qualified football team Clutch. We are going to state baby!!!"

My heart dropped. My teammates and cheerleaders walked in, filling the whole room up. My heart dropped again and again as they ran in. Louie was right, there wasn't enough room for all these people. Everyone tried hugging me but there were too many of them. Balloons, flowers, cards and small bears filled the room as well.

"Get well soon Clutch, we need you at state."

Louie told everyone I was really sick as he stormed in my room towards the window.

"Ok, take a look out the window for me."

The moment I got up to look, it felt like my heart fell out my chest. There were at least 200 people in the parking lot cheering. I waved to them all, feeling special, like a president or something, I felt so important. Some people really do care about me, even when I'm not on the field. I had time to bond with my teammates for a few hours while they visited.

The final score against Crandon High School was 14-8. I was asked one million times if I will be back for the state game. I told everyone the same thing, that nothing can hold me back.

After a while when everyone left I thought about Mom, I wonder where she is at this moment. I fell asleep that night with her on my mind.

As the days passed I was hungrier to get back on the field and run routes. I did pushups daily and Louie kept me updated on our playbook in case I'm cleared to play for state. I turned into a major football head in that hospital room. Some nights I would get set in my receiver stance acting like I was in the game, other nights I would toss my pillow in the air and grab it out of the air like it was a football. There's nothing wrong with me, I just needed a little time to rest.

It's the day before our state game and I'm nervous to hear my doctor's decision. Louie and I sat in the room patiently.

"There's one thing I want you to know Rajon," Louie said as he turned towards me.

"I'm listening Coach."

"Your mom has not been here to see you because I thought it would be best if she stay away for a while."

I stood up. "What?! Who the hell are you to control

what the hell my mamma does? Dude who do you think you are?"

Louie cut me off instantly.

"She's doing drugs Rajon," Louie said.

I stood there confused before deciding to sit down in complete shock, I lost all my choice of words. I'm confused and Louie couldn't even look at me in my eyes anymore.

"How do you know this?" I asked. The doctor walked in as I wiped my face.

"Mr. Rodgers how are you feeling buddy?" he said.

"I'm good Doc," I replied.

He questioned me about my ability. He tested me on dizziness, memory, and all sorts of other things. My mind is everywhere at the moment, Dee Dee, Mark, my grandma, Mom, and the state game.

At this moment I don't even care about living. My doctor suggested that I get at least two more days of rest. I didn't have anything to say, I didn't stand a chance to look at him or reply. Sitting at the end of my bed with my arms rested on my knees, I don't want to be bothered by anyone in the world, except my little sister. Louie tried talking to me but didn't get a response out of me. He offered me to come and watch the state game, but I mugged at him.

"Follow your heart Son," Louie said as he walked out.

I laid in the bed for the rest of the day, and no one got a response out of me in that place. It was almost like I was dead but my eyes were open.

Gram High was the school we are scheduled to face in state. There's no doubt in my mind that my doctor doesn't affiliate with Gram High. It doesn't even matter anymore, I'm just dead to everyone.

I checked on Dee Dee once today, no improvement at all. I went to sleep at 11:40 hoping I wouldn't ever wake up again, I even asked God not to wake me up. The next morning was a new feeling. I dreamed I heard a whisper from God in my dreams, He said, *You have No Limits Rajon. Be true to your heart, go catch your dream Son...*

I felt something, not just the words of God but I felt a new motive. I felt like God directed me into the right direction and gave me the strength that I've been searching for. I got out of bed with a purpose.

There are five hours before the game. We always practiced and warmed up before going off to a game, so I knew I had time to make it to the school. I got dressed swiftly, kissing Dee Dee on the forehead, and rushing out. I left my doctor a note on my bed. I'm pretty sure he would understand once he read it:

Sometimes in life all it really takes is a fall from the mountain to realize what you are climbing for. - Clutch.

I walked fast through the hospital hallways

ready for business. Being outside felt weird, I felt like a caged animal that has been locked up for years. I ran all the way home holding my keys in my left hand, pretending like I was holding a ball in the fourth quarter with the game on the line. I ran as fast as I could and switched the imaginary ball after every cut I made on the busy street between cars and people. As I got close, people knew what I was running for, some cheered me on. I rushed upstairs quickly to get dressed into my game day appeal, it took me 12 minutes tops. The moment I made it downstairs there was a car waiting for me, it was Lance, Dee Dee's father.

"You need to save that energy for the field Speedy, get in."

  A smirk appeared on my face as I rushed into his old school jeep. He drove kind of in a rush, knowing this game was important to not only me, but everyone who was coming to watch. All I could think about was the state game, I was ready. We stopped at a red light a couple blocks down. I peered out the window and spotted a familiar face on the streets, it was Mom, she looked terrible.

"Wait! Stop the car!" I yelled.

  I almost fell apart as I got out approaching her, Lance got out grabbing me to get back in the car. I don't think Mom even noticed me standing there but I didn't have the strength to call her name. She looked at me when I got back into the car, we made strong eye contact for a few seconds before pulling off. I'm mentally disturbed on the inside but I need to regain focus and pull myself together before I have another break down, I feel it coming. However, if one more thing happens, it might take me out. I revisited the words God shared with me and cleared my head for a moment which brought me back together. We made it to the school three minutes later.

"Yo Rajon, leave a mark out on that field today, don't worry about nothing but scoring and bringing a win back home with you. Do it for your city, but most important, do it for you and Dee Dee," Lance said

Before hitting the switch to unlock his doors to let me out, I shook his hand and got out. I had what he said on my mind.

My team was on the field in their game jerseys. Everyone looked the part from my point of view, even the coaches, everyone was adorned in black and gold amd the coaches in collared shirts with black hats. It made me more anxious to get dressed. My uniform was resting in front of my locker, I got dressed in less than 15 minutes but I didn't want to rush. I threw up before going out to the field which made me feel somewhat better. I came out of the building jogging towards my team with confidence. Everyone stood and clapped as I got closer, they even tried to do some type of group hug which was kind of weird to me.

"Y'all wanna cuddle or do y'all wanna go win state?"

Louie already knows why I'm here, he gave me

140

a genuine nod. I can tell from his facial expression that he was ready for business, just business. We all filled the buses at once, helmets and shoulder pads in one hand and our team duffel bag in the other.

The stadium where we were playing was one hour and 10 minutes away. The first game is being held at the University of Illinois located all the way in Champaign. My heart rushed as we pulled into two big black gates and we cleared the bus once we stopped.

"Good luck guys," the bus driver said as he opened the doors for us.

Our fans were already there waiting on us to arrive, they cheered us on as we got off. Only two hours and 15 minutes before game time. I'm not even nervous, nor do I have butterflies. I have no time for weak emotions, I'm just ready to play. I stayed to myself to mentally prepare.

Gram High was on the other side of the field playing around. In my head, they take us as a joke, so that made me even madder, someone from Gram High is going to pay. My teammates were throwing around footballs and studying their playbook. Louie came over and gave me the plays, I knew some of them already but I like what I'm seeing though. There are a lot of deep routes and trick plays.

"Coach I'm hungry," I said as I slammed the book closed.

"You didn't get a chance to eat this morning Son?"

Louie replied.

"No, I want the ball Coach, I'm hungry to win Coach."

"We will get you the ball, best believe we will, don't worry about that, just focus," Louie said as he walked off.

Time went by fast, 45 minutes until game time. We stretched for a while then went over the plays. Afterwards, we headed into a locker room when there were 15 minutes left on the board. We're fully dressed and ready for game time. While waiting, we all gathered and focused in on the coaches. Pre-game speech is what you can call it. After our lecture, the coaches talked to the side as we remained quiet and focused. I looked around and saw a few guys focused, some looked like they were scared, and some looked ready. As for myself, I'm just eager to get out on the field again.

I stood up and faced my team and said:

"You guys are my motivation. I've never had a real, actual family, I've had a few people get up and walk out of my life but I've been with you guys for four long years. This is what I can call my real family. In this cold world, you need a family, individuals to depend on. I lean on you guys more than you guys lean on me. I haven't given up because I know someone, somewhere is looking up and leaning to me on this team.

"We are here for one reason and one reason only: forget all your problems for these four quarters, forget the things that haunt you the most and focus on a once- in- a- lifetime opportunity. For the seniors, we will never ever play high school football again, this is your last game in high school playing this sport. This is a very good opportunity and a unique moment, and for some of us this is it period! You might have to hang up the cleats after today, I'm just being honest. A few of us might not make it to see 20, a few might be doctors, and a few might be drug dealers, whatever the case may be, this is it.

"You wanna leave a mark to the point that even if you be on the streets, you can wear your state championship ring and let all the young athletes know how it feels to be a state champion. It starts right now by finding your heart.

"Everyone close your eyes and find your heart. Dig deep and ask yourself why you are here. What did you do to get here? God has brought you here and He has *never made a mistake.* What do you want to accomplish today? My heart was bruised hours ago but I found hope, I found a will to wanna be successful and move forward towards my dreams! We can win this game today with heart, sometimes talent is not good enough. Heart is something special.

"Now open your eyes and look at the person next to you. He's your brother, he's what makes this family a whole and he's leaning on you today, he needs you. The moment you give up on a play, you are giving up on your brother. You might not see him next month, this could be his last day on earth. The last thing he did was depend on you. I'm letting you guys know I'm willing to lie down and die on this field today. I don't know who, I don't know his name, I don't know his jersey number, I don't know his mamma's name, but somebody, somebody gon' get this work today! Get yo ass up!!! It's game time! Go yo ass home if you scared, let's bring it up, give it your all today guys. Let's bring it home baby. Heart on three, heart on three. One, two, three-"

"HEART!!!"

We rushed out of the gate waiting for an entrance. Blood rushing through my body, anxious is not even the word to use at this point in my life. I'm itching to play, I'm fearless, I fear no one. I'm bold, I will do the honor of striking first in this game. I'm a dog, I'm a beast, I'm a lion, and I'm a gorilla. I'm just ready to score multiple times.

We rushed out to the field all at once. Fans were screaming to the top of their lungs, it's loud, and the bleachers are filled. I see my name in the crowd, signs were held up with my face on them, it was an amazing feeling. This felt like a college football game with all the people around cheering. I tried not to get too amazed, I kept myself focused on one goal. I kept a frown on my face the whole entire time before kickoff.

During the coin flip I glared into the eyes of each and every one of Gram High captains' eyes. I shook their hands with a firm grip. Their captains were tall and muscular, dressed in yellow and blue uniforms from their helmet to the stud of their cleats. Their quarterback favor, a Tim Tebow wanna-be. He's number 15, meaning he just might be a slight problem.

Sike! He's a dead man walking on this field. I have no fear from the size of these guys, matter of fact, I want their best defensive player guarding me. They won the coin toss and asked to receive the ball. We ran back to our sideline ready to go and get pumped up. I needed a quick moment to myself so I walked off and took a knee with my head down. Prayer is a conversation with God and I felt like I needed it.

I spoke to myself and God, "This is it, Grandma I know you're watching, I will not let you down. You prepared me for moments like this. I'm here now, this is my moment, my state championship. Thank you God for protecting me through all evil and hatred, I need You today. I need You every day, please stay with me throughout every play and bless my ability to perform in the correct manner. I love you Grandma, save me a spot up there. I love You God, rest in peace Mark. Amen."

Coach Louie came over and grabbed my face mask.

"Look at me, you are tough, you were made for a game like this. You've been through a lot these past few months I know that, but if you weren't tough, you wouldn't be here right now. Life has tried its best to beat you down, but you found a way to fight back. I need you today Son, leave your mark."

I can tell how bad Louie wanted this game, I think I want it more than he does though. I don't want anyone else saying anything else to me, I don't need anyone to preach to me, just put the ball in my hands and watch me glow. Players filled the field, it's about that time. The ball was kicked, Gram High let it go out of bounds, and the ball is on their 22- yard line. I just might to go in at safety.

"Be ready Clutch," Coach White yelled.

That means I'll be going in to play safety soon. Gram High was physical, they ran the ball hard at us, play after play gaining more and more yards. We were weak on our left side and they ran the ball that way three plays in a row.

"Coach I see the weakness," I said to White.

"On the next play go fill in that open gap that he's running through on the left side," he replied.

Next play I was in the game, standing in the back field calling out the plays. I was hoping for a pass but I had a strong feeling they were running the ball next play. I stood just a little deep to dare Gram High to make a quick run. Next I was creeping up to the line to welcome their running back to state. I twisted things my way telling our defensive end to go inside as I went out, we were hoping to confuse Gram High offense.

I met their running back one -on -one in a brutal collision. My head was ringing but I made the play in the back field. The ball came out but it was recovered by Gram High. I hopped up, eager beating on my chest. I felt dizzy for a few seconds but I pulled through with a clear vision. The sound of the yelling crowd made it all better, I just have a feeling Nicole is watching and I hope she saw what I just did. Second and 15 it was time to play smart now. I was being watched by their whole offense as I was creeping up slowly to make Gram's quarterback think I was rushing him again.

"Watch number one!" Their coach yelled out from the sideline.

      The moment I saw the ball snapped, I took off in the opposite direction looking for it. I knew this fake Tim Tebow wanna-be wasn't so smart. He literally threw the ball down field like I wasn't going to attack it. I turned into a ball hawk, grabbing it out of the air keeping my balance. I ran down field towards the end zone with ease. Making players miss, I wanted to score badly. I made it all the way to the five before taking a hard hit. Jumping up beating on my chest, I'm even more pumped up now. I felt like I had this game in my hands. Two big plays already and offense hasn't even taken the field yet. My helmet was smacked repeatedly by my teammates. That's just the football way of saying "good job."

      Offense took the field and Louie let me stay in the game. I don't need a break. We ran the ball up the middle twice before Bertron scored on a QB keep for the first score of the game, 7-0. After kickoff Coach White took me off defense, he wanted me to rest before going back in on offense.

Gram High scored on a 60- yard run by number fifteen. If I was in the game that would not have happened, I would've knocked his head off. They went for two but didn't make it, the score is 7-6 and it's time for kick return. Louie wanted me in the back field deep to receive. The ball was kicked, it looked like it was going far so I kept skipping backwards, focusing on the ball. It hit the ground before bouncing towards me. I scooped it up and took a stride down the middle then I bounced out towards the sideline, making defenders run into each other.

Gram High's special team had no chance against me. My team blocked perfectly leaving Gram High players on their knees. Ninety- two -yard kick return for a Lion touchdown. I feel good. The score became 14-6 in the first quarter with 9:17 on the clock. It came down to a dog fight later in the second quarter. The score remained the same, although I have a small issue: my left shoulder feels dislocated and it stings like hell. The Trainers took me into their room with three minutes on the clock before half. I'm pissed, but for some reason I thought about Mom. When I was little, she always came to rescue me whenever I got hurt. It felt like I needed her the most at this moment. I sat on a long table as they rotated my shoulder and wrapped it. I held some ice to it then Louie walked in during half time to check on me.

"How you feeling Son?" Louie asked.

"I'm good Coach, did anyone else score after I left?" I replied.

The trainer cut Louie off.

"His shoulder is going to need some rest Coach, a few more big hits will have his arm almost hanging off in the morning."

"What? It's just a damn bruise, I'm good."

Louie took a deep breath as he looked at me.

"Well I guess it'll just have to hang then because I'm not folding," I said as I got up and grabbed my shoulder pads.

I'm not trying to hear anything from anybody, I'm playing in this game during the second half by any means. Someone will have to kill and drag me off this field today if they think I'm going to quit.

I went into the locker room where my team rested. I told everyone I'm good as I walked in to prevent any questions. I sat there with an intense look on my face, I don't feel like talking. I'm just ready to get back out there and keep playing. Time ticked down, five minutes before it's time for kick return.

We all filled the field to stretch. I tried to stretch my shoulder the best way I could, I only felt just a little pain. Time ran out and it's the start of the third quarter, we're receiving the ball.

"PJ you're in, get deep and bring it on home," Louie

said.

"Coach!" I yelled.

"Clutch take a rest we're gonna need you healthy in the fourth," Louie said.

I didn't even trip. I just knew the moment I got back in the game I was going to execute. I stood on the sideline to watch, I didn't feel like sitting on the bench. The bench is never my place to be unless I'm waiting for Coach Louie to bring me a toy.

Gram High kicked off and the ball traveled until it reached PJ. He had a decent return, all the way to midfield. Offense then took the field. Another receiver filled in my spot as I watched from the side. I looked over in the crowd to spot Nicole, she was looking right at me. I looked away the moment we made eye contact.

I watched their defense the whole time, seeing what plays would be safe to run on our side of the ball. Gram managed to stop us after a few plays. Bertron looked kind of nervous as Louie called special teams to the field, so we attempted a field goal.

The score became 17-6. A few moments later Gram's offense took the field, they fought for yards play after play. Travis almost came up with a clutch interception, but he dropped it, that would've given us a little breathing room. They later managed to score on a 45- yard touchdown pass to a tall receiver. After their PAT, the score became 17-13, they're down by four. The third quarter was another gamble, 3:26 left on the clock and Louie still hasn't put me back in the game. The crowd has been yelling my name since the start of third.

"Put Clutch in" was all you heard.

With seconds left in the third, the score board didn't change one bit.

The start of the fourth was what I was waiting for.

"Get ready Clutch," Louie yelled.

I stood up and put on my helmet. This is the best feeling I've felt in a very long time. Everyone held up four fingers in the air to represent the fourth quarter. It's time to really get down to business. This is the last quarter of my high school football career. Gram High punted two minutes after the fourth began.

"Let's get it," I yelled to the top of my lungs.

Louie came over with Bertron.

"Ok here we go guys, were running fast tempo, everything is quick and crisp, four plays in a row, let's score on one of them. We're going Trips right tight X, Z quick, run that back to back, two plays in a row. Third play we're running up the middle with a 22 dive. Last two plays fake X, Z quick YW fades. Stay in trips the whole time, let's execute!"

We took the field quickly and lined up in trips not waiting on Gram defense. The ball snapped, I took a jab step forward and came back towards the ball. The moment I caught it, it was clutch time. I traveled the field preparing myself for anything. I made the first three guys miss from a simple juke move. I cut back after seeing too many Gram jerseys in my way, I wanted to score badly. I was out numbered two against one, a Gram corner and free safety. I ran out of bounds at the 42- yard line, I have to keep Gram High defenders away from my shoulder. We need 58 more yards to reach the end zone. We got set quick again. Same play, same pass, to the same guy.

"Number one Rajon Rodgers for a clutch touchdown."

That was all you heard baby.

That was my third touchdown of the game and I wanted more. Feed me until I throw up! When our defense came in, Coach White put me back in at safety. I had fire in my eyes. Gram High knew they needed to score soon. With the score at 24-13, we had an 11-point lead on these chumps. Gram High running back ran the ball fast and physical, I could relate. We met on third down, I didn't really want to use my shoulder to make a tackle so I kind of made the play in my own style. I met their running back as he ran towards the sideline. I slammed him to the ground as we collided.

"Come getchu some Boa! " I yelled in his face as I hopped off him.

"I'm running yo ass over next time," he said.

"You better come with some heat 'cause ain't no fear in my heart," I said as I walked back to the huddle.

This guy has another thing coming if he thinks he's running over me. Coach White took me out the next play. Gram put the ball in the air the moment I got out, it was another Gram High touchdown. White knew he made a bad decision. They went for two points and failed again. They would've been better on kicking a field goal for an extra point. The score became 26-22 and it's a dog fight with 5:43 left in the fourth. Our only choice was to fight and that's exactly what we did.

The first play went to PJ, he ended up gaining 15 yards on a quick slant. We ran the ball with Daniel and gained another first down. We're moving down the field, Gram High bumped their safety over to my side. I have two defenders guarding me while I ran a six- yard hitch route. Bertron put the ball in my hands quickly enough for me to make a play on that eager cornerback. I broke him down to one knee and gave him a stiff arm as I fought for more yards. His help was the safety, he took a weak shot at my feet that made me stumble for five extra yards before falling, but we got a 22- yard gain.

Time ticked down to 3:17 before Gram High called a timeout. Coach Louie wanted to play smart, he wanted to run some time down and get a score. He came up with a decent play that could possibly get us into the end zone, the famous route every cornerback can't stand: a stop and go route. I was anxious, this could be the play we needed. We got back on the field and I was confident. I looked towards the end zone as I got lined up. Gram High's main focus was stopping me,

I could just tell, the outside linebacker even bumped over towards my side. They were trying to get me three- on- one, but I'm making it one –on- one with that slow safety and me. That corner is good, but not good enough to guard me in a clutch moment like this one.

"Watch number one, watch number one!" Gram defense yelled.

As soon as the ball moved, I took off down field fast as I could. I chopped my feet hard, hesitating to come back to the ball, the corner and safety bit on it. I broke open free taking off up the field toward the end zone. Bertron threw the ball three yards ahead of me. I leaped and snagged it with one hand falling for six points. The crowd went extremely crazy but my sideline wasn't hyped at all. I noticed we had two flags lying on the ground.

"Holding on the offense," the ref announced.

My heart dropped and Gram's sideline celebrated. With only 2:02 left in the game we had 39 yards to go, we need to make a play fast. Gram High was even more focused on me. They put two corners on me with the safety over the top. Although it was kind of funny to me, I was ready to give out even more work. The ball was snapped, time ran down. The first corner tried to jam me at the line, I left him there, he's too slow. The second corner held onto my jersey a little, I managed to break free by smacking his hands off my jersey.

Bertron scrambled around trying to find me open, he threw a bullet into my chest on a cross route. I was hit hard by their middle linebacker the moment I caught it. The ball came out, my heart dropped the moment I didn't feel the ball in my possession. A Gram player recovered it and raced the opposite direction towards the end zone. I felt like my life was over when he got caught at the 10-yard line by Bertron. My shoulder is ringing with even more pain. Something is dislocated in my ligament area because my whole left arm is numb. I'm lying on the ground in pain. I tried un-strapping my helmet and gloves but I only could move my right arm. I think I'm out of luck. Time ticked down before the injury timeout. Trainers rushed the field. I got up on my own and stood on the sideline next to Louie.

"You're hurt Clutch, take a seat on the bench we got this one."

Those words played over and over again in my head as I looked around. There are 35 seconds left in this game, I must get back in this game although my shoulder is aching badly. The trainers wanted me to take off my shoulder pads so I could ice my left shoulder.

"I'm not taking off these pads until it's all zeroes on that score board," I said to the trainers loud and clear so they could leave me alone until this game is over.

Louie is out of timeouts, Gram High needed to score, and a field goal won't be enough to tie the game.

The state championship score reads 26-22 on the board, fourth quarter with 35 seconds left in the game. Coach White sent the defense out. He told me my shoulder was done. I stood there reminiscing about my high school career and everything that has happened to me in the last few months.

Something told me to look towards the stands, I think it was my conscience and I spotted Mom. She stood there in a dirty blue sweater gazing into my eyes. I reached deep into my sock reaching for the same piece of paper Louie gave me the day he neglected me when I was a child. Mom always told me I'll need that piece of paper someday. She told me to always keep it in my sock on game days. I walked up to Louie and grabbed his right hand putting the folded up piece of paper into his palm.

"Hold onto this for me, take a seat on the bench I got this," I said as I put on my helmet and ran out onto the field.

I told our safety to get out, I know I wasn't supposed to but I had no other choice. I wouldn't be able to live with the thought of myself not attempting to do something about this game. God told me to follow my heart and it has brought me to where I'm standing now. I heard Coach White yelling, but I paid him no mind. The crowd stood to their feet, they made it feel like an NFL Super Bowl game. It was beyond loud.

Gram High was 10 yards away from a victory and it was up to us to bring this game home. Gram High players took the field. The ball was snapped and their quarterback dropped back looking for an open receiver, he scrambled and took off towards the end zone. He's stopped at the five- yard line by our linebackers. Gram used their last time out as well but they have time for one last play, they're five yards away.

Everything felt like it was moving in slow motion. I can hear my heart beating fast. That very moment I thought about everything bad that happened to me this year. I'm not in the best condition to tackle, but I'm drowned with anger and blind to my fears. Everything that I've been through defines who I am right now at this very moment. I saw the ball move from the ground into Gram's quarterback's hands. It was a sweep to the outside. I raced over fast as I could. I couldn't see clearly because of my watered eyes and I had no help. Next thing I know, I became one –on- one with Gram High's running back. He pointed at me as he ran towards me. I frowned the closer I got to him, this is the same guy that wants revenge from a previous play earlier in the game. We're both running like bulls towards each other but only one can win this dog fight. He's running like he wants this game, I'm running like this game is all I have. He lowered his shoulder running at me, I braced myself.

We met one yard before the goal line....

To be continued...

157

Epilogue

In the words of Rajon:

    Life is really all about a race. This race will determine who will survive and who will get left behind and forgotten about. What's so special about this race is everyone will be at the starting line but everyone will not finish. They tried to break me, but it only made me the person I am today. I wouldn't be as strong as I am now if I hadn't experience some life changing speed bumps. I hope that my vision gives someone hope. There's no limit in anything I want to do in life. I was once told I'll be dead at the age of 14 but I can't dwell on the things that have happened to me in the past, life goes on. Life has its own little way of knocking you down and expecting you to not get back up in a matter of time.

    There are plenty of people in this world that face the most terrifying problems daily, so never feel like you are the only one. I learned that you have to be strong and mentally tough through anything. Great character, a strong heart, confidence, dedication, and pride are important keys in life I had to use to open the doors for myself.

    Throughout my whole entire life, as a young man, I've learned how much people care about me. I take mental notes of how people treat me and the things they say to me. I've been let down and lied to my whole life constantly without even realizing it.

The greatest thing I've learned growing up is God has never left my side no matter what. Even if it felt like He has. He's been here through it all. He's the sunlight in my life when everything else seems dark. I lost some very important people in my life and my heart is damaged because of that, my feelings are bruised. I feel like an ancient car with flat tires, a bad engine and low gas. How do I continue to move forward with all the parts of me not functioning well?

I want to give up but I just refuse to be average. You can either give up in life, or you can leave a legacy and an inspiring story behind that might change minds, grab hearts and fill them with wisdom and ideas about moving forward. I'm not quitting, I'm too driven to fail mentally. I know what I want and it's in my heart. Don't give up in anything you do. There is someone, somewhere leaning on you. It's too easy to give up, everyone quits but I'm not everyone. I'm Rajon Rogers who they call Clutch. My mind is made

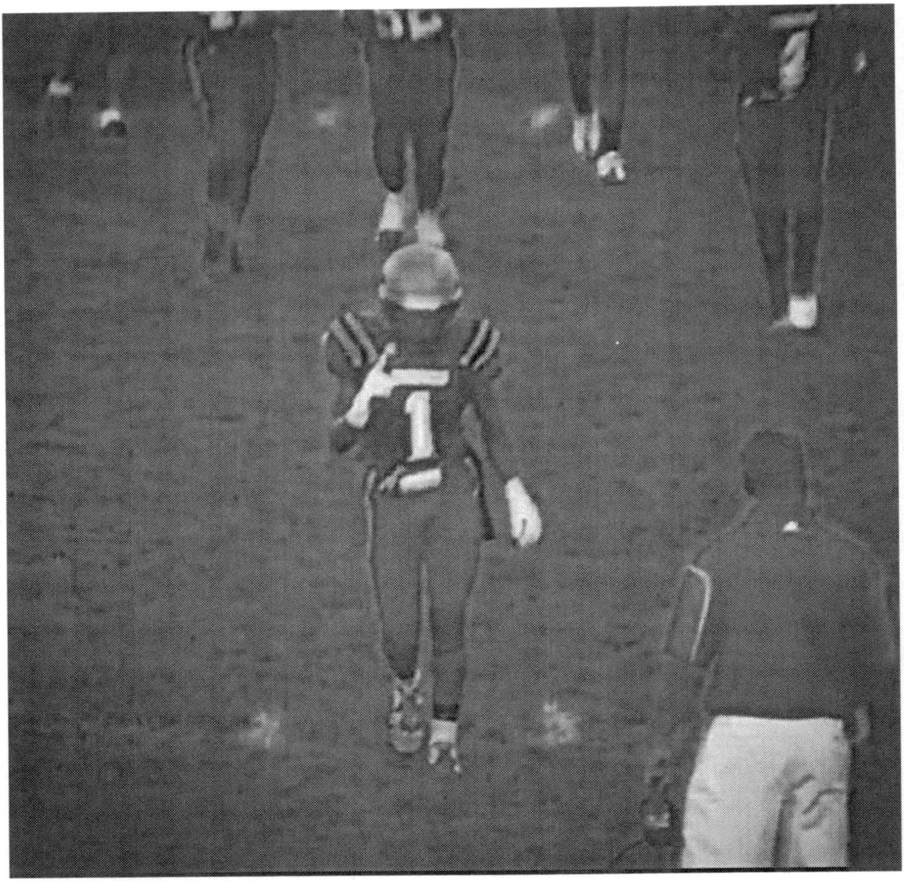

After Words

     I grew up in a rough neighborhood in Chicago, Illinois, but no one can tell that by the way I carry myself. It's a major difference between being raised around the hood versus letting the hood raise you.

     I wrote this book with passion, pain, experience and with every inch of heart. Rajon is a fictional character that lives through me, he's almost like my alter ego. Although I created him, it's like he still motivates me to want to become a better person and a better athlete.

Some days when I don't feel like getting out of bed I think, what would Rajon do? Then I hop right out of bed and get my day started seeking for success in anything I do.

I started playing football when I was in fifth grade. When I stepped onto the field I couldn't name a position or teach the proper techniques to any position there was. The only thing I knew how to do was run into anybody, full speed to see who falls first. The majority of the time I was the one who laid the big hit. When I was knocked down, I was eager to get back up and go hit somebody else.

     After the sixth grade I became more serious with football. I felt like football offered a path to a better life even though my grandma and mother always took very good care of me. In the seventh grade I became a second string defensive end that competed for playing time.

     September 12th, 2009 was a day I'll never forget. I had a championship game on my birthday. That was the only game my mother could attend because of her work schedule. I stood on the sidelines with a clean jersey the whole entire game except the last four minutes of the fourth quarter. My mother never got to see me put big hits on people. That day I told myself that I'll never stand on another sideline ever again and be forgotten about and I meant that.

I trained a way that I've never trained before and I did workouts that I wouldn't have ever imagined. I got up early in the morning to drink egg yolk and take a jog to a high school track that was a few miles away from my home. I ran up and down the bleachers until I wasn't able to stand up straight, I ran up and down the field like I was playing in the game during fourth quarter.

The next season I became the starting defensive end and the second string quarterback. In the year of 2011, I became a freshmen in high school and attended a school called Thornwood. I was number one and the starting quarterback. After my season, I was awarded the Most Valuable Player. After the season I trained even harder; even when there was snow on the ground and it was 20 degrees. I was still outside doing cone drills and running routes trying to improve myself.

The next season I remained the starting quarterback and I played free safety towards the end of the season. That season I was awarded the Most Valuable Player, I also won the award Offensive Player of the Year. After my sophomore year I switched to receiver. I hit a major speed bump and was affected by a dislocation of my shoulder. I prayed for better days and cried at night because of my absence on the football field.

My senior year I transferred to a school that was less than 10 minutes away from my home called Thornridge which was my rivalry. Thornridge didn't win a game on varsity in the last four years before I got there.

I was asked by many people over and over again why would I leave Thornwood to come to a losing school? I told everyone the same exact thing and that was to be an underdog and make a difference. When I transferred in it felt like home.

The people at that school would always comment that I was the new kid. All I heard in the beginning of the school year during football season was that I was the new kid from Thornwood.

After the season, we managed to win a few games and I earned an athletic scholarship to a Division Two university. My former teammates from Thornwood highlighted me as the best player on the team but I remained humble throughout the entire season and I wrote, "don't believe the hype," on my social medias. In fact, I didn't even want to be a captain because I didn't want to attract too much attention to myself.

My whole objective of writing this book was to motivate and influence others to never give up on anything in life even if it seems like you're at a dead end, keep pushing. The most important advice that I give to all my readers is "fit out." That means be different from everyone else.

When I wake up in the morning I look at life like everyone in the world is wearing an invisible black shirt. As I prepare for my day I put on my invisible blue shirt. The generation today is what motivates me to be a different, unique individual.

For information about Reilly, visit his social media pages at:

https://twitter.com/_Rjtheman

https://instagram.com/_rjtheman/

https://www.youtube.com/watch?v=3btddT0bmVs

https://ww.facebook.com/pages/Reilly-Jackson/504776946346971

Made in the USA
San Bernardino, CA
27 September 2015